W9-BSI-030

CONTENTS

Part I: Overthrow of the Status Quo

Part II: Taking It On the Road

Part III: Finding A New Normal

For my husband Michael,
who understands that life doesn't always
play out in a straight line.

INTRODUCTION

Life's most important journeys seldom begin at the beginning. They usually have their roots in an ending—a loss, a defeat, an ignominious meltdown. This book was birthed out of a midlife crisis, when everything around me came crashing down and life was not playing out as I had planned.

It was the mid '90s. I had hit my milestone 50th birthday. In the previous three years, I had faced Stage Four melanoma cancer, shingles, a major car accident at the hands of a drunk driver, the death of my dad, and the untimely death of my 42-year-old best friend. I was newly married to a man with a chronic illness and working as a mid-level executive for a nearly billion-dollar healthcare conglomerate going through a messy, exhausting merger.

I kept telling myself "I can handle this," until the day I couldn't. My husband at the time (now deceased) suggested I drop out of life for a while, to get away from all the "shoulds" and "oughts," and find a new starting point for the rest of my life.

Thus began my unscripted wandering alone on America's backroads. No cell phone, no GPS, no laptop, no itinerary—talking to strangers about their lives, wrestling with God about my own life.

I didn't have words for it at the time, but, in hindsight, I was looking for insights and answers to those gnawing core questions we all ask and answer at various points in our lives and then ask again when life does not behave according to our script:

- What's the point of life?
- What does God want?
- Who am I, really?
- Now what?

I thought finding answers would change everything. It did, but not in ways I expected.

In the years since the trip, I've met hundreds of people asking the same questions. If you're one of them, then you're one of the reasons I wrote this book. Take the journey with me. Perhaps your own answers will emerge. We're all just beggars leading other beggars to the bread.

Verla Wallace
Naples, Florida

ACKNOWLEDGEMENTS

I'm deeply indebted to the many people who helped advance this book along its circuitous path to publication. Some are no longer in my life due to time and circumstance, Others will be with me to the end. We need both kinds of people in our lives.

For those early encouragers who offered help in a variety of ways, my deep thanks to Kathy Woodliff, Ron Williamson, Kirk Niemczyk, Nancy Matheson Burns, Carol Fuys, Bob Biegon, and Mike and Ellen Sullivan.

I'm equally grateful for those who read versions of the book and offered their wise counsel, critique, and encouragement. They include my devoted husband Michael Wallace, my wise daughter Lisa Martinson, Dave Fessenden, Judy Keene, Eric Hamilton, Beth Krusich, Kathy Woodliff, Helena Madsen, Loretta Tulke, LaVonne Neff, Joe Durepos, Lyn Cryderman, Wes Roberts, and Deborah Lawrence.

My extended family and women's small groups also provided ongoing unwavering support.

A special thanks to Dan Landbo, who went above and beyond to create a beautiful cover design that captures the essence of the book.

Finally, I want to thank you, the reader, for choosing this book. If there was one enduring lesson learned from my trip, it's the value of listening to one another's story. Stories move us, teach us, remind us, and grow us. Sharing our stories can lighten the load and carry us further than we might ever go on our own.

I look forward to reading *your* story.

Trip Route

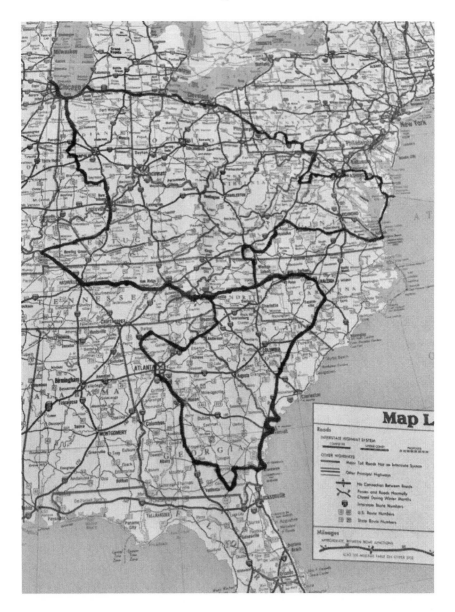

Chapter 1

**"It was the best of times, it was
the worst of times; it was the
spring of hope, it was the winter
of despair. "**

Charles Dickens
Tale of Two Cities

MELTDOWN

8 p.m.

I gave a smile and a nod to the security guard as I headed to the parking lot. Another 12-hour day working in middle management for a nearly billion-dollar health-care conglomerate.

America was crying out for health-care reform in the wake of skyrocketing medical costs. The health care industry was scrambling to consolidate, as a hedge against the feared arrival of managed care. My employer and their biggest competitor had entered into serious merger talks, hoping to ensure their joint survival and continued dominance in a crowded field.

We all knew if the merger succeeded, job cuts were inevitable. They wouldn't need two people at every position. So, employees daily marinated in the toxic air of paranoia and executives began to jump ship, including my boss who resigned and took two key managers with her.

It gutted our department's management team and I was tapped to take her place. I turned it down. The position didn't play to my

1

strengths and I didn't want to work for the person who would have been my new boss. He was furious.

"Why would you turn down an opportunity to advance?" he asked. "Aren't you committed to the success of the company? It's important that our management team look strong and competent so our department will be the one still standing when the ink is dry on the merger."

He insisted the merger was just weeks away. If I would ride out the storm, I could then give my notice, receive a glowing recommendation, and everyone would be happy. He promised to start looking immediately for a permanent replacement. Reluctantly, I agreed to take the job.

Another co-worker and I assumed the workload of five managers and the supervision of a dwindling team of subordinates.

The merger hit snag after snag. More staffers left. The workload increased. Then senior management decided there would be no new hires or recruitment efforts—even in mission-critical positions—until after the merger. I began to rethink my decision to stay.

Our offices were on the campus of a Level 1 Trauma Center. As I crossed the parking lot on this particular night, I glanced at the glowing red EMERGENCY sign that graced the back entrance and thought, with a bit of amusement, "We're all killing ourselves under the watchful eye of a healthcare institution devoted to wellness. Go figure."

I slipped into the car, reached out to put my key in the ignition, and my arm fell limp at my side like a rag doll. No matter how hard I tried, I couldn't lift it. I was 100 yards from help and couldn't move. It was as if everything shut down at once.

Eventually, my shouts brought a guard to my aide, but my brain was so fatigued I couldn't remember my phone number to call home.

Once home, after my husband George retrieved me, I fell into bed fully dressed and slept 20 straight hours without moving.

The next day sitting in the doctor's office with my husband, my doctor spoke bluntly. I had had a physical breakdown. And there were ulcers and other suspected issues, which more tests would confirm.

"I seldom get this dramatic," he said, "but if you don't quit your job, you face the likelihood of an early death. Your choice." George agreed.

I agreed, too. I had never felt so completely undone physically, mentally and emotionally. I promised to quit but said I needed to give 30 days' notice because it was the "right thing to do." My team had worked hard and given me their full support during a difficult time. I couldn't just walk out. In hindsight, it was a ridiculous decision.

Fortunately, after I gave my 30 days' notice, my boss was so furious he couldn't wait to hasten my departure. He waited just long enough for me to update the operations manual for our department and then, without warning, sent security guards to my office to permanently escort me from the building.

Chapter 2

"What does not satisfy when
we find it is not what we're
looking for."

C. S. Lewis

SEPTEMBER RECKONING

I stared at the calendar on the refrigerator. My self-imposed six-month sabbatical was about to end. My health was returning, but I had no clue what to do next. None of the options seemed to fit anymore. It wasn't about a job anymore; it was about getting a life.

The phone rang. It was Brad, an old friend who was president of a small consulting firm with whom I had occasionally worked as a subcontractor since leaving my corporate job. He wanted to let me know about an open management position in the offices of one of his clients.

"You've said you were going back to work after your health sabbatical. This job has your name written all over it. Check it out. I recommended you."

We exchanged pleasantries and I promised to stay in touch. The knot in my stomach tightened as I hung up the phone. I fought back tears as I pushed aside my soggy bowl of cereal.

My husband's chronic health condition had taken an unexpected bad turn and his long-successful small business was in serious trouble from a rash of new competitors. Financially, I needed to get back to work.

George walked in from the bedroom and poured himself a glass of orange juice. Noticing my tears, he sat down and put his arm around me.

"Honey, what's wrong?" he said.

"I can't do it." The words came out in a pained whisper.

"Do what?"

"I can't go back."

"What do you mean?"

"I can't go back to work!" I said, as if pleading for clemency. "Something's changed. I don't know why or how it happened, but something's wrong and I don't know how to fix it."

He looked me squarely in the eye and let out a deep sigh, "You know, there's been something on my mind for a couple weeks that I haven't known how to bring it up. Maybe this is the time." He braced for what he assumed would be news I didn't want to hear.

"I don't think this is about a job," he said quietly. "I think you're a woman warring over what's important and how you want to spend the rest of your life. You planned this comfortable life that doesn't rock any boats, but in the end you've followed the script that others have written for you. Dutiful. Responsible.

"The truth is," he said, "I don't think this tidy persona is you. There's this other woman—the woman I fell in love with, by the way—who keeps trying to 'break out.' But you keep stuffing her down for fear she might offend someone—especially you. She has strong ideas that never get expressed because they may upset people or challenge their assumptions. I know they're there because they slip out every now and then. She's passionate about important issues and doesn't tolerate fools. That Verla is

6

demanding a hearing and she's not going to shut up until you pay attention to what she's saying."

"That's easy for you to say," I shot back. "It's always been easy for you to break the rules. All those outrageous stories about how you hopped a tramp freighter to Brazil one summer as a teenager…or how in art school you stayed up all night to paint and hung out in jazz clubs playing your saxophone. Very existential. Mr. Free Spirit. But admit it! Even *you* finally realized you couldn't live like that and eat, too."

He nodded in agreement.

"What did you tell me you did after that motorcycle accident?" I said defiantly. "You settled down, went to law school, and played Mr. Button Down Guy like the rest of us. So don't talk to me abut 'breaking out!'"

"You're right." The sadness in his voice was palpable. "Six months in a body cast took me down a few pegs. A predictable life didn't look so bad after all. I did what everybody told me I should do. But look at me!"

His voice broke. "My art school professors said I had more talent than Jackson Pollock and all I ever wanted to do was paint! But did I paint? No. I went to law school. Why? Because my father went to law school and my brother went to law school. And I was told I was 'too smart to waste my life on art.' So for years I litigated cases 80-90 hours a week until I wrecked my health and was forced to find a career I liked even less than law, in order to support my family. Don't you see? I don't want you to end up the same way! You can still do something about it." His words brought no consolation.

"The bottom line is that I'm a chicken," I said in desperation. "For all my youthful vows of wanting to make a difference and not to settle for an ordinary life, I'm not like you. After life knocked me around a bit, I settled for *safe*. I'm allergic to risk. I like our predictable life. I like the fact that we can go out to a

7

restaurant when we want and take a trip when we want. I don't want to start over in some crummy walk-up apartment, living on ramen noodles in order to chase some impossible dream! What if I discover my purpose (or whatever you want to call it) is to be a great musician or dig wells in some Third World country? It's a little late to do that, don't you think? I'm 50!

He stood up to signal an intermission.

"Look, let's get dressed and head over to the park. If we have to talk about hard things, we might as well do it outside in the sunshine."

*　　*　　*

It was September but felt like a perfect spring day. Young mothers monitored their preschoolers playing on the jungle gym. A little girl in a pink sweatsuit put her Schnauzer in the sling of a tot swing and began to push the dog higher and higher. The dog wore a terrified expression as if to say, "How did I get here?" I felt the same way.

George and I sat lost in thought as I absentmindedly fed breadcrumbs to the birds.

"Maybe it's not time to make a decision about a job," he finally said, chewing on a blade of grass. "Maybe something else has to happen first. What if you were to do something totally different— like put yourself in unfamiliar territory where some of your assumptions about life could be challenged?

"Events of the last few years have kept you in 'coping' mode most of the time. What about going on the offensive and doing something for the sheer joy of it—without regard to whether it made sense or was practical or cost-effective or age-appropriate. Something with no grand purpose or timetable."

"Like what?" I asked.

"I don't know," he replied. "What would you *like* to do if money and family responsibilities weren't an issue?"

My mind raced. "Well, you know I love to travel. I like hiking around in the woods shooting nature pictures. I love to write...or used to. I don't do much of it anymore. Dad always said writers were dreamers and the rest of us had to work for a living. I've often wondered what my life would have looked like if that buried writer's 'voice' had found the light of day."

I interrupted my own monologue. "Look, this kind of daydreaming doesn't pay the mortgage. And talking about it only makes me more frustrated."

"Humor me," he said. "What else?"

"Okay, but this is making me nervous." I stood up to stretch and then plopped down against a maple tree to resume my rant.

"I'm mad. I should have bounced back by now and I haven't. Instead, it feels like I'm dying a slow revolting death. I want it to stop!"

"What if you were to take a road trip?" George said, as if he hadn't heard a word I said.

"A road trip? Where?"

"That's up to you. Where would you like to go?"

"C'mon! That's the last thing we have money for right now."

He leaned in close to make sure he had my undivided attention. "That's exactly why it's a good idea. You are so disgustingly responsible, it will take a big risk to cut you loose from all the 'shoulds' and 'oughts' that have shackled your life."

"It sounds like you want me to throw all my values overboard. I like being a responsible person."

"I like that about you, too, honey. I'm not suggesting you become a serial killer. This is about facing down your fears and finding courage. It's about subjecting yourself to risk and seeing what you're made of. Taking the trip feels scary, right? But if you

9

did it and found out the world didn't collapse around you, it might free you to take other risks and make other choices."

I hated to admit it made sense.

"This is not a joke, right?" I said. "You're really serious that you'd support this? Because we could end up in a financial bind for a while if I don't find a job right away when I get back." I let out a deep sigh. "I can't believe I'm even entertaining this."

He seized the opening. "We'll probably have to put some of the trip expenses on plastic. But, to me, it's an acceptable risk because it could change your life. You don't have to know how something will end in order for you to begin."

Inexplicably, the conversation ended. For reasons neither of us quite understood, the matter seemed settled.

We drove home; I grabbed a calculator and the checkbook and began crunching numbers. If I took the trip, how long could we meet our obligations with existing funds after I returned? Where could we borrow money if I didn't find a job right away? What kind of interest rate would we pay if we charged some of the trip on a credit card? I had never paid credit card interest in my life. It was a personal badge of honor. I felt like throwing up.

We agreed on lifestyle changes that would stretch existing cash as long as possible—no eating out, lots of macaroni and cheese, only essential purchases and a drastically scaled-down Christmas.

We set ground rules for talking about the trip once it was over. No blaming the trip for hard times that might follow. No second-guessing the wisdom of taking the trip. No pressure for the trip to provide answers. Maybe it wouldn't. We both fell silent. The implications piled up in my mind.

*　*　*

We waited a week to let the plan gel before going public about the trip. We agreed if either of us had a change of heart we would abandon the idea and never mention it again. A week later I called my mother.

"Hi, Mother! Just wanted to let you know about a trip I'm planning."

"That's great, honey. Where are you and George going?"

"George isn't going. I'm going alone."

Long pause.

"Is everything all right, dear? How does George feel about this?"

"He's fine. He's the one who encouraged me to do it."

"It…it sounds wonderful," she said, trying to sound supportive. "I wish I had the nerve to do something like that. I would be afraid something would happen and I wouldn't know what to do. When are you leaving?"

"As soon as I get organized. The car gets a full inspection tomorrow."

"Where are you going first?"

"I don't know. Maybe I'll flip a coin. Heads, I go east and tails, west. Can you believe this is your daughter talking? Miss Never-Make-a-Move-Without-Her-Day-Timer?"

"I'll be praying for you, dear," she said, sounding totally unconvinced. "I'll check in with George to hear how it's going. Send me a postcard when you get a chance."

Jenny was next on the list. Ten years younger than me, her life as a nurse, mother of six and a foster parent to a cocaine-addicted infant, didn't leave her much time for dreaming about taking off on an adventure. I felt a little guilty telling her of my plans.

"I'm jealous!" she interrupted. "Don't get me wrong. You know I love my life. Paul and the kids mean the world to me. But sometimes," she sighed, "I wish we could 'drop out' for a day to catch our breath, you know? We still talk about taking off three months to hike the Appalachian Trail—just the two of us. I hope we can do it before we get too old."

11

In all the years we had been friends, I never knew about her dream to hike the Trail.

To my surprise, every person on my list gave the trip a thumbs-up. The idea seemed to strike a universal nerve. Not a single zinger about me having a mid-life crisis. One husband joked I was setting a dangerous precedent for his wife, but he urged me to "go for it" anyway.

Preparations began in earnest. My seven-year-old car received two new tires, an emergency road kit, warm blanket for the trunk, and a canister of pepper spray to put under the front seat for added protection. I placed an extra set of car keys in a magnetic key holder under a bumper.

The hoots began when I bought a clunky key ring—the kind that hooks onto a pant loop—to eliminate digging in my purse for keys. George warned that the fashion police might arrest me for Felonious Impersonation of a Janitor.

I packed for every conceivable scenario. A small overnight bag held the basic essentials. It would be the bag I carried into the motel room each night. A much bigger suitcase would remain in the trunk and serve as the "closet" from which I'd restock my daily clothes, minimizing the amount of loading and unloading required every night.

My adult daughter, Lisa, who could live out of a duffel bag for a year if necessary, was mortified.

"Ma, you're not going to a Third World Country! Why are you taking so much stuff? There'll probably be a Wal-Mart five minutes from wherever you are."

"Wait till you see what else I'm packing," I whispered.

I filled a large canvas bag with books, magazines, an atlas, my Bible, and journal. Another large gym bag held bottled water, fruit, rice cakes, pretzels, a can opener, Swiss army knife, Baggies, napkins and plastic forks, and spoons. An additional tote bag included a stack of my favorite CDs, 36 rolls of film, and my camera gear. I felt fearless—ready to "go where no man has ever been." Probably because no man would be caught dead with that much luggage.

*   *   *

The night before my departure I tossed and turned from the moment I crawled into bed. About 2 a.m. I rolled over on my back and stared at the ceiling in a panic.

"Can't sleep?" George said, vaguely aware I had pulled away from my usual nesting spot.

"What am I doing?" I waved my hands in the darkness with great flourish. "I must be out of my mind! This is not a business trip where you fly to another city, hail a cab to a hotel, sit through a boring meeting, and fly home. I'll probably end up in the middle of nowhere … in bad weather … in the dark. My car will break down, some Charles Manson-type guy will stop to help me, I'll point the pepper spray in the wrong direction and blind myself. This is a bad idea! **I'm not going**."

George sat up in bed, disoriented, trying to wake up enough to sound coherent. He rubbed his eyes and reached for his glasses. He never talked without his glasses on—even in the dark.

"Honey, if you drive out of the driveway and turn around and come right back, it's okay," he reassured me. "I promise not to make fun of you. You can be gone for two hours, two days, or two months. In fact, you don't have to go at all! But you've come this far. Why not see it through and see what happens?"

He yawned matter-of-factly, took off his glasses, rolled over and resumed a resonant snore.

The next morning I delayed the inevitable, leaving notes all over the house about when to water houseplants, how to defrost meat in the microwave, and other endless minutiae. After exhausting all stall tactics, I backed the car out of the garage and rolled down the window to kiss George goodbye. The sun backlit

13

his thick salt-and-pepper hair like some cheesy Hollywood movie scene. He looked taller than his 6'4" frame.

"It's going to be great!" he said. "Got your motor club card? Your debit card? Your library card?" he teased.

"Very funny," I said with a nervous smile. "You forgot to ask about my voter registration card." Slowly I pulled out onto the street and watched as he grew smaller in the rear-view mirror. My courage was gone before I reached the city limits.

Chapter 3

**"I'm always in a hurry to get things done,
I rush and I rush until life's no fun.
All I've really got to do is live or die,
But I'm always in a hurry and I don't
know why."**

*From a country music
song by Alabama*

LEAVING THE FAST TRACK

Despite a late start, I still hoped to cover a couple hundred miles before stopping for the night. It didn't look promising.

Eighteen-wheelers formed an unbroken caravan from Chicago's south side warehouse district toward I-80, the main east/west interstate for over-the-road truckers. Road construction and unending detours added to the misery. As I tediously rounded the southern tip of Lake Michigan, I had plenty of time to decide which direction I wanted to go.

Pioneers always traveled west to break new ground. I always assumed they only turned back east if they lost their way and needed to regain their bearings. That certainly fit my life. Instinctively, I turned east and then south, where people revere the past.

I didn't have a strategy beyond my plan to stay on backroads, take my time, ask a lot of questions of the people I met, and pay attention—not just to other people but also to God and to what my own life was trying to tell me.

*   *   *

Lafayette, Indiana is a nondescript college town with a vibe that implies, "You're welcome here but don't expect us to make a fuss." A billboard on the edge of town pictured a quaint motel that resembled an English Tudor castle. It touted budget prices with "all rooms on the first floor and your own private entrance."

Probably a charming bed-and-breakfast-type place. Perfect for my first night on the road.

Truth-in-advertising apparently didn't extend to billboards. The room reeked of cigar smoke, despite an ugly "No Smoking" sign on the wall. Dark drapes, hideous brown-flocked wallpaper, and 25-watt bulbs in the lamps created a brooding medieval atmosphere. A tiny television hung on a wall pedestal next to an oversized wall-mounted bottle opener.

I grabbed the plastic ice bucket and fled the room in search of vending machines.

Outside "my own private entrance," construction workers were polishing off several six-packs as they hung off the back of their pickup trucks. Their evening ritual apparently filled downtime during their extended stay, working on a nearby highway project.

"What's a purty little lady like you doing in a dump like this?" one asked. "Are you here to make our Happy Hour happy?"

"Aww, shaddup, Bill. You act like you're in heat. Why would she want to talk to a slime bucket like you?"

I smiled benignly without looking at them and kept on walking.

Neither of the deadbolts on my door worked, so I jammed a chair under the doorknob. After a fitful night's sleep, by 6:00 a.m. I was dressed and eager to leave. The pickup trucks were already gone.

*   *   *

White clapboard farmhouses, barns, and silos dotted the flat Indiana landscape. Red tractors crisscrossed endless fields of ripened corn and wheat. The fall harvest was in full swing. A hand-painted sign beside the road caught my attention:

Pumpkins, Jams, Pies For Sale
Amish Dolls   No Sundays

Farmers in Amish dress were gathering pumpkins in the adjacent field. I pulled off the road onto the shoulder to watch them, feeling like a voyeur peeking in on an Early American painting sprung to life.

A handsome man in white shirt, black pants, suspenders, and a wide-brimmed hat pulled his horse-drawn plow through the field. Across the footpath other Amish men worked alongside Amish women in their traditional long gray dresses and white bonnets. Methodically they worked the rows, selecting and loading pumpkins onto a flatbed hitched to a tractor.

Despite the backbreaking work in the midday sun, good-natured teasing sprinkled their conversation—borne, no doubt, of working many harvests together.

What is it about the Amish that's so unsettling? Is it their contentment? From what I've read about them, they don't seem to care if they're recognized or considered "important." They don't look for something outside themselves to assign them worth. They believe God made the earth and everything in it, so everything has value—including their own lives—regardless of what they choose to do for a living. Their satisfaction comes from mastery of the ordinary and faithfulness to the task at hand. Their plain lifestyle has never appealed to me. Yet, they're not out here hundreds of miles from home, trying to figure out who they want to be when they grow up. Points go to the Amish.

I extended my camera out the window as discreetly as possible to capture the slice of Americana. But, as soon as my lens appeared, all of them turned their backs in unison and headed for the barn, as if prompted by some unseen warning system. I quickly pulled away, embarrassed to have interrupted the rhythm of their lives.

At the local General Store down the road, I asked the proprietor why the Amish didn't want to be photographed.

"..goes against the Good Book," he said sternly. "Photographs are idolatry—'graven images' that compete with God. Ain't you ever seen their dolls? They've got no faces. They're the only folks in the U. S. of A. that don't want no 15 minutes of fame."

*   *   *

Red-faced men in John Deere caps crammed into the roadside café. Every person in the place followed me with their gaze as I sat down self-consciously at the only empty table. UFO sightings were apparently a more frequent occurrence than a woman dropping in alone for lunch at the rural equivalent of an all-male country club.

"Reggie, watch yer tongue, boy, lest that lady over thar' think we're un-CIV-il-ized. Keep that dead rabbit in your pocket." he deadpanned. Chuckles all around.

"Settle down, Jesse," his table partner chided. "What do you know about bein' civilized? You think a restaurant's good if there's a sign out front that says, "EAT HERE."

Local event announcements plastered the walls. A church event to honor Thelma Hutchins on the occasion of her 100th birthday. A Gospel Sing on Saturday night, featuring The Jeffries Family. A local insurance salesman promised, "a fair deal every time." Handwritten 3" x 5" cards advertised corn planters, combines, and a Chevy flatbed truck.

The handwritten menu offered 13 kinds of homemade pies, seven of which were already sold out. I ordered a piece of sugar cream pie and feigned disinterest in the farmers' table-to-table crosstalk about the weather, the crops, and a bull for sale.

"Bill, d'ya see that exercise video they was showing down at the hardware store." He whistled under his breath. "Whewww-eee! That girl on the tape don't look like any woman I ever met."

"Well, you old coot, those videos are for the ladies. Not for you!"

"Shoot, Mel, I bet Ralph got it just to drum up business. It's a lot more fun watchin' them girls jumpin' around than watching some demo on how to castrate your bull." More laughs.

Mel paused, summoning his best imitation of deep concern. "Well now, I'm worried that girl don't have enough meat on 'er bones to handle the winter cold." (Longer pause for effect.) "Ya think I ought to offer to share my long-johns with her?" The entire room erupted in hoots and hollers.

I quickly finished lunch and made my way to the cashier, hoping to slip out without notice.

"Honey, don't mind the boys," she said. "They ain't used to seeing ladies around here. You lookin' for antiques? We got lots of estate sales around here."

"No, I'm just passing through."

"All by yourself? Ain't you the brave one."

Back in the car I stifled a smile and realized there's a lot you can learn in places you're just "passing through."

* * *

The next morning I participated in a business conference call scheduled weeks before my trip dates were set. My consulting colleague had asked me to sit in on a brainstorming session for a major client project. It was a rare return to the corporate world since I'd left six months earlier.

Hotshots in three cities gathered around their speakerphones. A female vice president in Chicago moderated and kept us tightly focused on the ambitious agenda. She gave everyone a voice but no one a platform. I relished their intelligence and focus and found myself swept back into the adrenaline rush of making grand plans.

Then the irony of it all hit me. They were likely sitting at chic Herman Miller desks, sipping a Starbucks venti mocha latte, as they looked out onto spectacular city skylines, while I sat on the edge of a lumpy bed covered with a rocking horse bedspread, in a no-tell motel in rural Indiana.

We were a community of peers in many ways, despite our vastly different circumstances. Well, at least we were people who treated each other with professional respect and admiration. But somehow it didn't feel the same as the Amish working the pumpkin field together or the farmers who gathered for lunch at The Farmer's Table Cafe.

The deepest kind of relationships—the kind that feeds our soul— grows most easily in the soil of shared values and a shared passion rather than shared work. And figuring out how to live a purpose-filled life takes a lot more than whiteboards, brainstorming sessions, and a strategic plan.

* * *

The trip was supposed to slow me down and create space to entertain new thoughts, but the conference call snapped me back into overdrive.

Back on the road, my hopped-up mind searched like a magnet for something more to do. I scanned the radio dial in search of news and thumbed through my date book to make sure there were no forgotten appointments. Did I bring enough stamps? Did I remember to bring my doctor's phone number? Checking. Rechecking. Making lists. I was hundreds of miles from home with no one counting on me for anything, but unable to dial down the pace of my life.

I really don't know how to do this.

*　　*　　*

A long row of Peterbilts, Freightliners, and Kenworths stood side-by-side like diesel dominos at the rest stop, while their drivers enjoyed a smoke at nearby picnic tables.

I gathered trash from my car and stepped around a state trooper who was leaning against the trashcan, chatting it up with the rest stop janitor who was draped over a push broom.

They talked amicably about the weather, the mosquitoes, and their kids. The trooper worried that his brother wouldn't get his crops planted before the predicted early frost. The maintenance man complained he couldn't afford new tires for his 15-year old pickup.

Think slow.

"How many miles to Turkey Run State Park?" I asked the trooper.

"Oh, I reckon about a hunert miles," he said, "'cept you're going in the wrong direction." He tried hard to hide his smirk.

I let out a disgusted sigh.

"What's the problem?" he said, chewing away on his toothpick.

"I'm not from around here and I…"

"Oh, honey…I knew that," the trooper interrupted. "You're movin' way too fast for trash dumpin.'" He smiled and said gently, "You know, I'll bet the world would wait if you took 'er down a notch."

The maintenance man, sensing his friend's comment might not have been welcome, jumped in with directions.

"Lookee here, miss, just make a U-turn out of the parking lot and head back west till you hit the state road with the cemetery on the corner. Go due west about 50 miles and look for the Quik-Mart near Marshall. Folks there can get you the rest of the way."

I offered a weary thanks and an hour later pulled into the local gas station/mini-mart for information.

A heavyset woman with a ruffled apron acknowledged me with a nod and continued sweeping.

"Excuse me, I'm trying to get to Turkey Run. The small roads around here are confusing on the map. What's the best way to get there?"

"I'm not from around here, honey. Ask Sam."

Sam stepped out from behind the counter to restock the chewing tobacco. He said he didn't know Indiana had any turkey farms.

"It's not a turkey farm," I said. "It's a state park with a lodge. Turkey Run is its name."

"Lan' sakes, girl. Ya learn sumptin' new ever' day. Maybe the missus and me ought to check it out. Sorry, I cain't he'p ya. Need any gas?"

"No, thanks," I said. "But I'd like to use your ATM machine."

"Thuh whut?"

"You know, the bank machines that dispense money?"

"Cain't say I've ever seen one, hon, but I've only lived here 'bout five years. You'd best ask in town at the feed store or the Chamber of Commerce. They'd know more about that stuff."

I thanked him for his time, bought a small bottle of orange juice and a bag of pretzels and left with a major case of attitude.

What is it with these people? How can you not know about a major state park that's less than 20 miles away! And who in this day and age doesn't know about ATM machines?

* * *

The small, unpretentious lodge was nearly empty, which was fine with the hikers and nature lovers on hand who weren't eager for their favorite getaway destination to become too popular. Besides, it was midweek and the off-season.

I threw my bag in my room, grabbed my camera, and headed out to shoot a few pictures in the late afternoon sun. The front desk clerk recommended nearby Sunset Point and Rocky Hollow Falls

Canyon for its great view of the sandstone gorges carved out during the Ice Age.

Trees 20-30 feet tall grew sideways out of the rocks and then turned up as if pulled skyward by some unseen hand. A suspension bridge across the gorge swayed precariously in the wind.

When I approached the canyon, a scout leader was explaining to his young troop that the area had been a favorite fishing spot for the famous Indian Johnny Green and the Miami Indian tribe. "Johnny Green died fishing right over there on Goose Rock," he said.

The boys' faces registered their wonder. Awesome! Death by fishing! Their amazement turned to disinterest when they discovered that jumping up and down on the rickety suspension bridge was much more dangerous than fishing.

*   *   *

After supper, I curled up in one of the rattan rockers on the second-floor veranda and rocked mindlessly in silence as a light breeze rustled the trees. Stars crammed the sky, unhindered by ozone or city lights. Down below, a raccoon approached the young couple sitting on the front steps. Its ringed eyes looked like moving bull's eyes as he slinked in and out of the shadows, snooping for a handout.

This is another world. I've missed so much because I was paying attention to the wrong things.

*   *   *

Songbirds outside my window woke me the next morning. The clock read 11:00 a.m. I shot upright, shocked to have slept 12 hours straight. Bone-deep fatigue still pressed in on me like a heavy hand. I flopped back down on the bed and slept another two hours.

* * *

Parke County, Indiana's 32 covered bridges require ingenuity, serious walking shoes, and a good map. Once found, they're not all that fascinating unless you get excited about old barn-like structures differentiated only by their size and the inscriptions painted over either end:

Narrows Bridge, 1882, J. A. Britton, builder

Cox Ford Bridge, 1913, J. A. Britton, builder

**Billie Creek Bridge, 1895, J. J. Daniels, builder,
CROSS THIS BRIDGE AT A WALK**

*Maybe I'd care more if I knew these builders' stories. But without further information, the bridges just stand there like tired old men waiting to be noticed. Still, the bridges have lasted a hundred years. What have **I** built during my life that will be **my** legacy a hundred years from now?*

I stretched out on a grassy knoll and clicked through in my mind the people I've known who left a legacy worth remembering. Surprisingly, the first person to come to mind was my Grandma Gladys.

Life was hard in her tiny farmhouse in the Dust Bowl of Kansas following the Depression. She faced fierce poverty, marriage to a mean man, failed crops, and a stillborn child. But nothing bowed her indomitable spirit.

"You can change your circumstances," she would later say matter-of-factly, "or you can change your attitude toward the circumstances." Then, with a sly grin, she would add, "Of course, some of us get better circumstances than others."

Every summer a couple dozen grandkids and great-grandkids would vie for invitations to stay, in turns, at her one-bedroom farmhouse where temperatures routinely topped 100 degrees.

She raised chickens and hogs and Uncle Ralph farmed her fields. We were guests by only the loosest of definitions. We were more like extra farm hands, albeit pint-sized. Still, there was something magical about the place. We felt lucky to be there.

Wheat harvest was my favorite time. At dawn, I'd drag myself out to the fields to take up my post behind Uncle Ralph on his rusty old combine. For hours he would guide the frightening machine through the white-hot furnace of dancing wheat as the sun beat down and the wheat chaff spun into the air, gluing itself to our eyebrows, skin, and ears. It felt like important work.

Some years a drought or floods or tornadoes seized the wheat before its time. Farmers would gather at Dutch's Grocery Store, smoke Camels, and talk with vacant eyes about how it would be a tough winter. Maybe they wouldn't plant next season. Maybe they'd "hang it up" for good and take a job in the Delco factory over in Neodesha. For Grandma, it meant no new cloth coat and another year without indoor plumbing. She never shed a tear. She'd make do. She always did.

We kids were oblivious. All we knew were days filled with endless adventures we could retell all winter long to jealous city friends. Each night we climbed the rickety stairs to her attic (the barracks for kids-in-residence) to sleep in our underwear on mattresses laid end-to-end on the floor. A few faint wisps of air through the gabled windows offered meager relief from the unrelenting heat.

No one slept much. Well into the night, the older kids repeated family lore about Grandma and her family to wide-eyed younger cousins. We'd share how Grandpa died when I was six—single-handedly lifting a car off a man who had flipped it into a ditch near the farmhouse. After failing to save the man, Grandpa came home, sat down in his favorite chair, and died.

Then there was the story Grandma often told about her mother, who traveled west as a child on a wagon train. She stitched dollar bills into her little girls' petticoats to hide the family's savings, in case roaming renegades attacked.

My favorite story was Grandma's first serious act of teenage rebellion. She painted Uncle Dot's farmhouse floor bright red—out of spite—after Dot left her and Grandpa in charge of a failing farm while he sought a more prosperous homestead further west in Colorado.

Grandma worked harder than men twice her size and half her age. She was up before dawn to feed the chickens, gather eggs, and slop the hogs. Then came the enormous breakfast she prepared each day for the farmhands and assorted hangers-on who showed up at her table at 6 a.m. After the men left for the fields, cooking began all over again for the other meals of the day.

She could wield an ax with exquisite precision, chopping off the heads of endless unfortunate chickens destined for the lunch table, after the grandkids plucked off the smelly feathers—an onerous job from which there was no escape. Mounds of fried chicken accompanied giblet gravy, mashed potatoes, homemade biscuits, pole beans, and at least two kinds of pies.

Afternoons brought more chores, laundry, mending, and forays into town to pick up feed. Always something.

She loved to eavesdrop on her crank-up wall phone and listen to bickering neighbors who shared the line. With great delight, she would place her hand over the mouthpiece and report their arguments word for word. We felt like dangerous little spies.

After everyone went to bed, she'd sneak a bowl of homemade ice cream from the freezer, read her beloved *Capper's Weekly* and listen to "Fibber McGee and Molly" on the giant Philco radio that produced as much static as dialogue.

It wasn't much, but it was enough. I asked her once if she was happy. The question mystified her.

"Happy? Well, hon, I don't think about it much. I have work to do, enough to eat, and folks around me that I love. What more do I need?"

Grandma modeled hard work, love of family, contentment, and faithfulness to what God put in her hand to do.

*She built into **people** and she left a far more impressive legacy than these covered bridges.*

Chapter 4

**"Did you ever have the feeling you
turned into the wrong person?"**
*Blythe Danner in the movie
"Back When We Were Grownups"*

QUESTIONS

My daughter swears I was born with a question in both cheeks. I want to know things. On my tombstone they'll probably etch my final question: "Was this really necessary?"

Now, after three days on the road, the questions were piling up faster than answers.

How long will this take? Will the benefit outweigh the cost? How long will my family tolerate my absence? The trip seemed like such a crazy indulgence.

The question that I keep revisiting when life doesn't work out as planned is: "What's the point? What exactly is the point of my one-and-only life? As a Christian, I know the catechisms and creeds that say the chief end of Man is to love God and enjoy him forever and advance his purposes in the world. But what does that look like for *me, now* at *this* moment in my life?"

They're questions that even people ask who have no strong spiritual belief system. A cranky, disillusioned business colleague once told me, "I probably wouldn't push back so hard about this whole life purpose thing if life weren't so unyielding in its demands and stingy in its returns. But when life takes so much out of you, you want there to be a *point*, dammit!"

Most of us didn't expect it to be such a difficult question to answer. Fresh out of college, we had a long list of options for giving our lives meaning: marriage, family, career success, personal achievement, financial security, philanthropy or something else. And, if we didn't have a clue about what to order our lives around, there was no shortage of people willing to pick a life for us.

Dad wanted me to follow him into the business world. So, after graduating from college, I dutifully went into the business world.

My mother wanted me to marry some nice young man and become a suburban housewife. (It was the 60s and her role models were Ozzie and Harriet.) So I married a nice young man whom I barely knew, moved to the suburbs, and started a family.

One of my first bosses said I had the potential to be a business executive but needed to go to grad school and earn an MBA if I was to break the "glass ceiling." So I entered grad school on a scholarship until I finally realized it was his dream, not mine. My heart didn't want to be there. My story lay untold somewhere else.

The pattern went on for years—life choices made with no understanding of how or if they fit into any grand scheme of things. The only thing I learned along the way was that a lot of other people were in the same boat.

We don't see it coming. All we feel are the symptoms. (i.e. "I have no energy. I'm bored. I'm frustrated. Why am I here?"). Our lives aren't awful. They're just *beige*.

I wish there was a label for the condition. Then we could say, "Yes, my life is unfulfilling because I've developed a nasty case of Ambivalencia Confusionitis. But, not to worry. I've taken two self-help courses, one weekend retreat, and purchased a T-shirt with a nice thought on it. I should be back on my feet in no time."

Well-meaning friends said I lacked a Big Dream worth throwing my life behind. I didn't lack dreams. They were just dreams no one else understood, dreams I didn't know how to make a reality.

As a child, I dreamed of being Brenda Starr, the newspaper reporter in the comic strip. At that age it wasn't so much that I was passionate to write. I just thought that writers didn't have to make their bed or weed the garden and nobody minded that they asked lots of questions.

Or maybe I would write a great novel. When I was ten years old I wrote my first short story, "The Horse That Wore High Heels." It was two pages long. I thought it was thrilling. All that my teacher noticed was that I paragraphed incorrectly. My parents figured it was just another childhood fantasy that would eventually wane— like wanting to be Spiderman or Wonder Woman.

As an adult, I was told again and again the importance of setting aside childish things and becoming a Responsible Adult. But *words* set up camp inside my head and refused to leave until I put them on a page. Words filled my journals about what baby's breath smells like and why lightning bugs belonged *outside* of Mason jars, not inside. I ranted about what happens when we silence those with more to say than those who own the words.

When passion threatened to undo me, words hidden in my journal helped to quell the storm. When anger rose up and I wished I had a gun, writing about it saved me from doing hard time.

But my dad would always say, "Writing is for dreamers. Find something important to do, something that will make me proud."

After college I forged ahead in the business world, gravitating, without even realizing it, toward assignments that let me wrestle with words. I quickly learned the only words my bosses wanted to hear were words like *strategic alliances* and *value-added* and *empowerment*—words everyone repeated in unison, regardless of whether anyone believed them.

I played along, cranking out the correct words, until one day the words declared an insurrection. It happened during a simple assignment: Write a short speech for the boss to inform the rank-and-file about the business climate, financials, blah, blah, blah.

But, instead of the words The Suits expected, out popped jazzy anecdotes and bridge-burning calls to action. It wasn't supposed to happen.

"How come the VPs stared at me like that? " the Chief Suit asked. "All those compelling arguments made people press me for details. What were you thinking? We don't have details!"

"It's the words, sir," I sighed. "They need a voice. It's a problem I've had since I was ten. I'll try to make them behave." (That's actually not what I said, but it's what I thought.)

How did I miss in hindsight what now seems so patently obvious? Writing was in my DNA. I never gave it credence because I processed everything through a heavy veil of others' expectations and my own faulty filters. And none of them included writing.

I couldn't believe that something that makes my heart sing could possibly be linked to something as important and responsible-sounding as my life purpose. Dreams had to be *appropriate* and *important* and *impressive*, right? They had to generate a lot of money and come with a title. They required *permission*. And if they weren't understood or affirmed or applauded or financially practical, they surely must be abandoned.

I pressed on. I bought motivational tapes and books, took leadership retreats, and journaled my brains out, searching for the perfect formula for a *great* life—especially one that had God's stamp of approval.

Maybe there was a secret formula, right? We all love quick-fix formulas. An advertising executive once told me, "Honey, don't get hung up on the whole 'meaning' and purpose thing. Meaning lacks traction in our culture. Get yourself a formula that works. People love 'em. You know, like, 'Personal Satisfaction in Ten Minutes a Day' or 'Three Secrets to Happiness for Under a Hundred Dollars.'"

I believed him.

Maybe it's time to throw out the naive notion that life's important questions can be answered by a formula or a slogan on the back of a t-shirt.

In the movie, "A Few Good Men," actor Jack Nicholson's character sits on the witness stand in a military courtroom, undergoing fierce cross-examination by Tom Cruise's character. At one point Nicholson explodes in anger and says to Cruise, "What do you want from me?"

"I want the truth!" Cruise shouts.

"The truth? You can't handle the truth!" Nicholson replies.

Aww, sure we can, Jack. We've tried everything else.

Chapter 5

"What I really lack is to be clear in my mind what I am to do, not what I am to know ... to see what God really wishes me to do ... to find the idea for which I can live and die."

Soren Kierkegaard

COWBOYS AND THOROUGHBREDS

Seymour, Indiana's downtown business district was closed to traffic to accommodate the Oktoberfest crowds. Hundreds of people milled around food booths along the sidewalk where volunteers raised money for local church and fraternal organizations.

An amateur band punched out German polkas on one of the entertainment stages. The potbellied musicians in authentic lederhosen drank beer out of genuine German steins, their ability to have a good time far outstripping any musical prowess.

Harley-Davidsons ringed the beer garden near the stage like obedient watch guards. Inside the fenced enclosure, bikers in their obligatory bandanna, black leather jackets, pants, and boots, gathered to out-boast each other with road warrior stories.

"How much does one of these things cost?" I asked a biker as he hopped off his hog.

"About sixteen grand for the basic model," he said. "Some start at nineteen or twenty grand. I've got another $10,000 in mine for extras like the candy paint."

Some of the bikes had double seats that looked like living room sofas. I fingered the leather. "Pretty fancy. I've never seen one of these up close."

"You must not get around much, lady. We're America's last cowboys and we like our rides 'luxe.'"

"Don't cowboys wear hats anymore?" I teased. "None of you guys are wearing helmets. Or do you like the idea of scrambled eggs for brains if you wipe out?"

"It isn't cool to wear a helmet."

"Let me get this straight. You shell out $30,000 for the privilege of scraping bugs off your teeth and cheating death. And that's cool?"

"Hey, risk and freedom are what it's all about! While you're playing it safe in some wimpy suburban gas-guzzler, I'm living dangerously. Guess which one of us feels more alive?"

"Ahhh, the Zen biker?" I asked with a smile. His manicured fingernails and stylish haircut gave him away. "You don't seem the biker type. What do you do for a living?"

"Tax lawyer." He folded his arms and waited for my startled reaction. "Those guys at the end table over there? They're all CPAs. We ride together on weekends."

"You're kidding!"

"Louisville firm," he grinned. "Come Monday morning I'll be back fighting for 'Truth, Justice, and the American Way.' Is this a great country or what?"

I walked around examining the other bikes. "So you're only living your dream on weekends? If being a highway 'cowboy' is so great, why not hit the road 24/7? That's what I've done," I said, with more bravado than I felt.

"Can't afford it. How would I pay for my gear?" He pulled up his pants with a mock swagger. "Remember, I gotta stay 'cool.'"

"Now who's playing it safe?" I said.

"Checkmate!" He stuck out his hand for a shake. " Say, are you really on the road full-time? For how long?"

"Don't know. Now that I realize I don't have the proper wheels, I'll probably get thrown off the road as a fraud!"

"Not a chance," he said. "Out here it doesn't matter. Life on the road is different. People don't get hung up on labels. You never know who a person really is. You only know who they claim to be at the moment."

"Well, the world is already overpopulated with people trying to be someone they're not. I'm not one of them," I said. "I want to be myself. The problem is I'm not exactly sure who that is."

I stopped talking, self-conscious at my babbling on to a stranger. "Sorry. Didn't mean to go cosmic on you."

He waved off the apology. "No worries. On the road you can try out who you'd like to be and see how it fits," he said. "No one will know. Take a few risks. No one will see you fail. Plus, you have a front row seat to watch some of the most interesting people in the world and you don't even have to buy a ticket."

"Do you qualify?"

"Nah, I'm just out here having fun, trying to make sure all the serious stuff I do during the week doesn't ruin me." His voice trailed off as he searched for the right words. "If you're out here on the road long enough, though, you do learn to recognize those who have figured things out and those who haven't. The wise ones have found what makes them happy and feel no need to defend it to anybody. They could care less what the rest of us think of them. I envy them."

"Pretty serious talk for a beer fest," I said.

"Hey, I'll buy you a beer!"

"No, thanks. I plan to eat my way down Main Street and make it to Louisville before crashing for the night."

We shook hands and headed in separate directions.

I confess there's a certain appeal to the idea of 'trying out' who you want to be on strangers, without having to explain or defend yourself. But it implies we pick a persona like a Halloween costume, never planting your feet and declaring "This is me." Of course, that presumes you know who you are after you peel off all the expectations placed on you by family, friends, peers, and our culture. The real challenge is learning how to be authentically *you* in spite of all that.

I wandered through the crowd, sampling a "hog samich" (BBQ pork), Cajun pork rinds, Creole etoufee`, and a funnel cake. Two dollars bought a stroll with seven other people in a musical cakewalk and a chance to win Ida Mae's Carrot Cake with Burnt Sugar Frosting. I didn't win.

The warm still air felt more like a June summer night than late September. The friendly crowd made it hard to leave. As I drove out of the parking lot, the festival announcer blurted over the public address system, "It's 10:30 p.m. and 72 degrees! Ain't God good to Indiana?"

*   *   *

Driving in the darkness toward Louisville, the biker's words replayed in my mind like a taunt. A rush of memories came to mind of times in the past when I've panicked because I made a bold move and got an avalanche of pushback.

I remembered my early days in broadcasting when I was the newly minted Public Affairs Director for a Chicago network radio affiliate. I didn't know then that most on-air "talent" avoided public affairs positions like the plague because, unless you worked for National Public Radio, the shows were considered a career dead-end. Everyone wanted to be a news anchor or investigative reporter instead, in the center of the action. I was thrilled for the chance to be on the air in a major market, even in dead-end slots.

At that time the Federal Communications Commission required radio stations to devote a certain percentage of airtime to public service programming. But since those programs generated no ad revenues, stations typically dumped the shows into "gutter" hours like 5 a.m. on Sunday morning rather than prime hours when people actually listened. It was another reason no one wanted the job. No visibility.

I lobbied the program director for a better time slot and created a new program, arguing it was worth placing in the station's "prime time" hours. It would be a 5-part mini-series of 90-second segments that would run Monday through Friday in "drive-time" (morning and afternoon slots when many listeners were in their cars going to and from work). The series would address a different timely topic each week.

He didn't think it would work but gave me a month to test it and see how listeners reacted. "Don't bore me," he warned. "Move the needle." (Broadcast lingo from the days when an applause meter measured the response of a studio audience.)

My first mini-series was a hard-hitting primer on street drugs. It was early in the "war on drugs." Parents still believed drug users were ex-convicts—not honor students from the suburbs. Today that notion seems downright archaic.

It was an opportunity to educate parents and teens about PCP, angel dust, and other street drugs that—in today's high-risk drug culture and opioid crisis—seem tame.

The segments contained raw urban street sounds and compelling sound bites from average teens who talked anonymously and candidly about why they used drugs and how it changed them. Cops and psychologists weighed in, too.

My boss was nervous. "This is radio," he said. "Mothers are making peanut butter sandwiches and trying to get their kids off to school. They want the weather, a traffic report, and a little light banter to keep them company. They don't want to know Johnny may be scoring nickel bags of dope on his way to soccer practice."

In the end, he relented.

When the first segments hit the air, one of the first listeners to react was a paramedic who was the father of two young children. He called the station to tell me to go to hell.

In a full-blown rage, he said I was single-handedly responsible for giving young people an education in what drugs were "out there," along with the lingo to make it hip to use drugs. Thanks to me, he said, he expected to be picking ten-year-old kids out of gutters who had overdosed. He hoped I'd be fired.

My boss, on the other hand, was thrilled. It "moved the needle."

I realized now how much easier it would have been to pick some safe topic or not to take a strong stand. Like the Louisville biker, I could have dipped my toe into controversy to see how much pushback I got and then morphed my position into something more palatable. But that's the exact opposite of who I wanted to be. Unfortunately, somewhere along the line, I forgot.

Note to self: People-pleasing and worrying what people think are not pillars to a satisfying life.

*   *   *

It was nearly midnight when I reached Louisville. My arrival coincided with two of the city's biggest events of the year—a major square dance convention and one of the nation's largest art festivals. All the motel rooms outside the city along the interstate were booked.

After an hour fighting Louisville's intricate expressway interchanges in search of lodging, I was angry and exhausted. I begged a desk clerk to recommend anyplace in the area that might have a vacancy. Minutes later I stood in the lobby of an urban high-rise motel whose best days had come and gone. Despite the grim lobby, the price was right. I checked in and fell into bed without ever opening my overnight bag.

*   *   *

The next morning the deafening roar woke me with an adrenaline rush. It sounded like an invading army of tanks on the hotel roof. I slipped out of bed and peered around the heavy drapes to see an unending chain of semi-trucks barreling across the overpass almost directly overhead.

I turned on the light and tried to focus. In the cruel light of day, the room was a joke. What wasn't plastic or fake was broken. The dime store pictures on the walls were all crooked, presumably because of vibrations caused by trucks rumbling overhead.

Traveling on the cheap is a drag. I know this isn't a vacation, but I'm about three minutes away from ditching this stupid trip.

I stumbled into the bathroom for a quick shower. The small ceiling light connected to a fan with decibel levels that rivaled a jet engine. I debated whether to take a shower in the dark or risk a migraine from the ear-splitting noise. Between the fan and the overhead trucks, I figured my hearing would be gone within the hour. I checked out as quickly as possible.

*   *   *

The desk clerk suggested a visit to nearby Churchill Downs before leaving Louisville. My original plan was to avoid tourist attractions but I convinced myself this was history. The historic landmark is the oldest continuously operated racetrack in America. Besides, there would be horses. I love horses.

The track was closed for the season but the Derby Museum remained open to accommodate tourists. Exhibits included serious-as-a-heart-attack instructions for how to make a proper mint julep and the chance to weigh yourself on a traditional jockey scale. An autumn haze cast an eerie spell over the empty racetrack and grounds. I walked around the empty courtyard studying the names of Derby winners displayed like a wallpaper border.

A clean-cut teenager sat eating his lunch near a statue of Aristides, the first Derby winner.

"Donerail won in 1913," he said, squinting against the sun. "He was the greatest long-shot winner who ever ran the Derby. He was considered such an unlikely winner that even his trainer didn't bet on him. And over there to the right? That's Broker's Tip. The Derby was the only race he ever ran. They called it the Fighting Finish Derby because his jockey and another jockey started horsewhipping *each other* during the race instead of their horses!"

"How do you know all that?" I asked.

"Aww, it's part of the spiel," he said matter-of-factly. "I'm one of the tour guides. But I already knew a lot of it."

"Sounds like you enjoy your job."

"It's about as much fun as you can have and still be legal! I can't imagine doing anything else. I love history and I'm a talker and a storyteller, so it's a good fit. My whole family's got Derby in its blood. My granddaddy worked here as a groom. My aunt sold tickets. I've lived near the track my whole life."

He looked at his watch and leaped to his feet. "Man, I'm late! I'm supposed to take out the next group!"

"Is the tour worth taking?"

"Heck," he grinned sheepishly, "you just heard my best lines! But if you want to see a live thoroughbred before you leave, go take a look over there at Deputy Joe." He pointed to a fenced pen with a small horse barn.

"We keep him around for the tour groups. Technically, you're not supposed to be wandering around on your own, but tell the groom I said it was okay. I'll be over there in a minute with my group."

Deputy Joe was not an actual Derby winner. Derby winners are too high-strung and valuable to be subjected to tourist "show and tell" several times a day. The thoroughbred's claim to fame was his aristocratic lineage. He was the great-great grandson of 1964 Derby winner Native Dancer, which made him worth hundreds of thousands of dollars and rescued him from the glue factory.

As a tour group walked up behind me, Deputy Joe's handler launched into his canned speech about champion thoroughbreds. He pulled back the horse's upper lip to reveal a tattooed registration number that identifies the horse if it's ever stolen and eventually recovered.

"If all thoroughbreds have 'the right stuff' because of their bloodline," I asked, "what makes one horse a champion and others like Deputy Joe just 'also-rans?'"

"Derby winners run like they're claiming their inheritance," he said. "They understand they're royalty. They know they're special, and they don't let anything get in their way."

The majestic horse stood patiently beside his handler as the tourists lined up to take pictures. I hated seeing the magnificent animal treated like a freak show attraction. If the handler was right, old Joe was born with everything he needed to be a champion but the horse just didn't believe it. That missing piece permanently relegated him to a lesser life.

If the analogy holds true for humans as well, then I have everything I need in order to be who God made me to be. The raw material is already there to do what he created me to do. But it doesn't do any good if I don't claim my inheritance. God, don't let me end up like Deputy Joe.

* * *

The *Louisville Sentinel* reported that 650 artists were exhibiting in the St. James Court Art Show, one of the top juried art shows in the country. I didn't want to spend another night in Louisville but had a couple hours to kill before I needed to hit the road. The lawyer/biker in Seymour had said, "Watch the people you meet. They'll tell you a lot."

Maybe it's time to watch a few artists.

The photographic exhibits drew my immediate attention. One exhibitor explained unapologetically that he earned his living as an ecologist, although his first love was photography. Rather than seeing his job as a conflict with his heart, he saw it as a great marriage of passion and profession.

His job required him to visit some of the country's most scenic destinations. With careful planning, he could coincide work assignments to each destination's peak natural beauty, creating prime opportunities to indulge his passion for nature photography.

He visited the Blue Ridge Mountains when dogwood trees were in full bloom. He arranged a trip to Tucson when thousands of cacti at the Saguaro National Monument were in full bloom. In the Pacific Northwest, he captured Mt. Rainier's snow peaks at their most breathtaking.

Being in the right place at the right time—factoring in his creative eye, special filters, and lenses—he performed his job and had time left over to create jaw-dropping scenic images.

At another booth, an architecture photographer displayed photos of the interiors of famous public buildings taken from different angles. He linked the photographs together in companion panels, giving the viewer the sense of standing in the middle of a 360-degree scene. I studied the pictures, marveling at the convincing illusion.

"This guarantees I won't be pursuing photography as a career anytime soon," I muttered.

The photographer overheard my lament.

"Why not?" he said, amused by my response.

"I'm a total dud when it comes to the technical tricks that create this kind of 'wow' factor," I said. "I just take pictures. I have an intuitive sense of how to compose a shot and people seem to like the results, but I can't explain what I do. I just know. But it definitely involves no technical wizardry."

"So maybe you're the other kind of photographer."

"What kind is that?"

"Some photographers—like me—are technical nerds. We drool over precise f-stops and the perfect toner for printing our pictures. The other kind of photographer is more of an artist. His eye and gift of composition are his strengths. He looks for a certain moment or a look. You've probably heard of the famous photographer, Henri Cartier-Bresson?"

"Of course!"

"He was an artist/photographer. He used to say, 'I don't think about it. Something just captures my attention—a facial expression, a leaf that evokes a feeling, a scene that tells a story without a word spoken.' Guys like him see things that I don't see. They don't worry about the perfect f-stop. They're editorializing."

"Once you knew what kind of photographer you were, how did you know what to do with it?" I asked.

He look surprised that I wouldn't know.

"Just start where you are. Find something you love doing and keep doing it. Let it grow on you. Pay attention to whether you *keep* liking it and whether you get better at it. Don't make your primary consideration whether you can earn a living at it or if you can afford to do it full-time. It has value, even if it isn't how you pay the bills. Just start. Ignore what other people think about what you're doing or whether you're using your college degree.

"Pretty soon the work will take on a life of its own," he continued. "It will tell you where to go. The question of what to do will have been answered. Then the question will be, 'Do I have the guts to do it?' By the time that happens, the satisfaction will have hooked you and the battle is over. You'll do it because you can't stand not to."

"You make it sound so simple," I said.

"The process *is* simple. Doing it is another story. That's what separates the men from the boys. I admit if I'd known how hard it would be to get to this place, I never would have done it. I had to stop trying to figure out all the angles and solve all the problems. You never will. The 'what-ifs' will sink you. There are tradeoffs.

But if you're willing to follow your gut and not give up, you'll get there. You *will* get there.

Chapter 6

**"It is necessary now and then for a man
to go away by himself and experience
loneliness, to sit on a rock in the forest
and to ask of himself, 'Who am I and
where have I been and where am I going?'"**
*Carl Sandburg in a 1950s
magazine interview*

ESCAPE INTO THE QUIET

Outside my door, honking ducks roused me from a deep sleep. I didn't order their wake-up call, but my room was only a short waddle from the edge of Lake Barkley.

I wrapped myself in a blanket and moved onto the tiny porch to enjoy the ducks and the water lapping against the shoreline.

The remote state park lodge in western Kentucky was a perfect hideout. Like Turkey Run State Park, it was the off-season and the place was nearly deserted.

For the next three days I ate, slept, walked the trails, and steadily worked through my self-assigned "homework"—sorting out my values, what mattered to me, what were my "must haves" and "can't stands," my legacy to date (or lack of one), and whatever lost dreams I could remember.

*   *   *

Midway through the soul-searching I took a break and drove to nearby Land Between the Lakes, sandwiched between Lake Barkley and Lake Kentucky. The landlocked island in the middle of nowhere is one of America's 40 official biospheres, used primarily for ecological research and conservation.

Its scruffy landscape was hardly scenic—at least not in the traditional sense. But it had a certain appealing wildness.

A modest nature center housed coyotes, owls, and hawks in their natural habitat. Docents dispensed arcane information that didn't exactly make your heart race. (A barn owl can turn its heads 180 degrees and catch up to 100 rats a night. Who knew?) But it was a welcome change from hours spent pondering the meaning of life.

Each night I settled back into my spot on the patio outside my room, listening to the crickets and watching fish break the lake's surface. One night a raccoon—close enough to touch—peered at me in the darkness, trying to discern if the human statue looking back at him was friend or foe.

A different cast of characters takes over the woods at night. As I sat silently eavesdropping on their world, I wondered if they were doing the same on mine. I soaked up the solitude like I was on life support.

I've never been a quiet person. I understand the value of silence, but it's not a natural part of my DNA, at least not yet. Growing up, the only time our house was quiet was if no one was home. We're a family of talkers—often all at the same time.

I suppose that it should have come as no surprise, then, that I drifted into broadcasting (albeit accidentally) and then into public speaking. Talking, talking, more talking.

Nature speaks in a loud voice at night—the crickets, the night owls, the rustle of trees, but I'm wordless. No one seems to miss my lack of contribution to the racket. With no words and no audience, I'm forced instead to listen. You learn more from listening than talking.

* * *

Despite brief nightly calls home to report on my travels and latest whereabouts, I missed the predictable routine and familiarity of family and friends—especially those times of the week when all of us were typically together.

On Sunday morning, loneliness swamped me. I pulled out the Yellow Pages to find a church service to attend. Dozens of churches (more than 30 Baptist churches alone) existed within a short drive of the lodge. This was definitely God-country.

* * *

I nearly missed the turnoff to the church nestled down in a "holler." A modest cross-shaped sign at the top of a narrow gravel road was the only tip-off. Pickup trucks and 10-year old cars filled the makeshift parking lot. Children darted between the cars, playing tag.

The church looked like a tiny prefab house with the interior walls knocked out. Inside the bare bones structure, about 20-30 people began to congregate, sitting on folding chairs in front of a makeshift pulpit.

I dressed down for the occasion, but there was no mistaking who was the outsider. The women wore undistinguished catalog-style cotton dresses. The men, in western shirts and string ties, sported farmer tans—dark brown faces with white foreheads where their tractor caps rested the other six days of the week. It made their heads look about a quart low.

Several people warmly greeted me and made small talk in a not-too-subtle attempt to learn where I was from and why I was there alone. I was then handed me off to the pastor's wife, a woman of genuine warmth, who sought with great diplomacy to ascertain my spiritual condition.

I suspected the course of these people's lives had been determined more by geography, education (or lack of it), and family tradition rather than choice. They drew a shorter stick than me.

But, if that's the case, then where I live or what I do for a living is not the benchmark of a well-lived life. It simply represents the location and circumstances of my life—not its purpose. I want something more.

A man with an accordion and Elvis-style pompadour stood up and led the congregation through a rousing medley of gospel songs. The short, balding pastor joined in from the sidelines with his tambourine and a high-stepping jig.

After the offering, the pastor announced his sermon would be about King Solomon's search for the meaning of life.

Is this some kind of celestial humor, God? You plop me in Nowhereville to tee up a sermon just for me? Cute. Real cute.

"King Solomon had it all," the pastor began with great fanfare. "He was handsome and rich. He lived in fancy palaces. Food, wine, pleasure? You name it. Hundreds of wives served his every need."

A shy grin formed on the pastor's face. "Let's just say no one's headache ever interfered with his plans." Chuckles rippled through the room.

"He wrote thousands of songs and wise sayings. You can read many of them yourself in the Book of Proverbs. If anyone knew the secret to a happy life, it was old King Solomon."

Then the preacher leaned forward as if to share terrible news.

"But brothers and sisters...ohhhh, dear brothers and sisters...listen to the sad words of the great king."

"Yet when I surveyed all that my hands had done and what I had toiled to achieve, everything was meaningless, a chasing after the wind. "
Eccl. 2:11 (NIV)

The attentive listeners responded. "Well, all right then." "Amen." "C'mon now." "Preach it, brother."

"A man wants to know his life means something," he said, thumping his finger on the podium in righteous indignation. "No one wants to come to the end of the road and find out his life didn't matter."

The talkback grew more enthusiastic.

"But, wait! Dear friends, the king didn't give up! He kept looking until he finally figured it out. It's right there in the Good Book. Check it out in Ecclesiastes:

"God has set eternity in the hearts of men."
Eccl 3:11 (NIV)

The excited preacher began to pace the platform. "Do ya' hear that, friends? God wired us for a different time and place so we'd never forget where we came from and where we're going. Money and fancy cars and houses are the currency of this world. But they aren't big enough to satisfy people who have eternity in their hearts!" He could barely contain himself.

"Some of us thought this was home and we've been trying to get comfortable here ever since! But, friends, our hearts know better. This isn't the main event! The real action is up ahead."

The audience murmurs rose to an appreciative crescendo. The congregation began a final song as the pastor invited his small flock to "do business with God."

I slipped out the back door, not wanting to give away how the country preacher's simple words had slipped right past my well-honed defensive filters, right into my heart.

I hurried back to my room and flopped onto the bed.

My heart is calibrated for eternity. That's why it can't be satisfied with anything not linked to eternity. That's why I get so bored with new experiences after a while and why one more achievement just doesn't do it for me anymore. God, it's like you buried a microchip in me that makes my life work the best when I'm in tune with your plans and not my own agenda.

I slid down off the bed onto the carpet to talk to God, to tell him how sorry I was for missing the point all these years.

* * *

The peacefulness of Lake Barkley refused to loosen its grip. I lingered one last day for a final round of picture taking.

A waitress in the lodge dining room suggested I check out the nearby town of Cadiz and stop by Little River that ran through town. "Keep an eye out for Duck Man," she said. "He hangs out by the river and he likes meetin' folks from away."

There was no movie theater or bowling alley in Cadiz and the closest dinner restaurant was 20 minutes away. Its most exciting retail store sold an odd mix of blue jeans and used sequin gowns for 30% off. I tried to imagine why anyone in Cadiz would need a sequined gown.

Little River wound through the city's park, a park by only the loosest of definitions. It was easy to find. I parked, threw my camera over my shoulder, and scrambled down the riverbank to stretch out in the afternoon sun and watch the clouds roll by—a pastime unpracticed since I was a 10-year-old Camp Fire Girl working on my cloud badge.

An old-timer backed his pickup truck and boat rig onto the makeshift boat ramp and then rolled the boat, trailer and all, into the water. Once offloaded, he pulled out his rig and tipped his hat as he tied up the pulleys.

"Howdy, ma'am. Nice day for pictures."

"…sure is! Do you come here often to fish?" I asked.

"Well, let's see." He took off his cap, wiped his forehead on his sleeve and rolled his eyes skyward. "I reckon this is my 76th year."

"You're 76 years old!"

"Naw, this is my 76th year of fishin' in Little River."

"Really? You must know all the best spots. What's your secret?"

He cocked his head in mock seriousness. "Get here yesterday! The best fishing is always the day before I get here." He let out a deep-throated cackle. "Lan' sakes, girl. No one goes fishin' to catch fish!"

"They don't? Then why do they fish?"

He leaned against his truck and pulled out a wad of Skoal, tucking it in his jaw. "Aww, I suppose it gives folks a chance to hum or think or reminisce, without havin' to report to nobody. These days everybody reports their feelings to everybody else— their po-LIT-i-cal feelings, their sex life, the state of their finances, and what they ate for breakfast. All that jawin' can wear a person out." He let out a deep sigh.

"Sitting out there in the cove with a line over the side? Well...there ain't nobody interested in your sex life out there, ya see. It's just you and the fish and the trees and all. And when you think of somethin' you gotta do, you realize you're stuck in the middle of a river! Whatever was so all-fired important can probably wait."

With that, he hitched up his jeans and hopped into the boat. One sharp jerk on the engine's cord and he was on his way downstream.

"Have a nice sit, little lady," he shouted from the boat. "I bet you can't do that where you come from."

I laid back into the sweet-smelling grass.

So true, old man. So true.

The midday heat created a luminous haze over the water. On the opposite riverbank, ducks swam between branches of a weeping willow that hung out over the water. On my side of the river, dozens more ducks begin to gather, as if summoned by an invisible magnet.

A white minivan tore into the clearing beside the river and the driver blasted his horn. The ducks waddled toward the van at breakneck speed, falling all over each other to get there first.

A gray-haired Black man climbed out with the aid of a walking stick and began talking to the ducks as he pulled scoops of dried corn and chunks of Wonder Bread from the back of his van.

"All right now. There's plenty for everybody," he said patiently. "Just settle down. You act like you ain't seen food in weeks. C'mon, stop biting each other."

The man's grandson scrambled over the back seat to help distribute the food.

I shot several photos from a distance and then walked slowly toward the van to avoid startling the ducks. My caution was unnecessary. The ducks were not interested in anyone but the man with dinner.

As I approached, he introduced himself by name but said everyone called him Duck Man.

Twelve years ago he'd been a machinist up north until unexpected surgery for a brain tumor left him partly paralyzed on one side, forcing his early retirement. He and his wife moved to Cadiz because it was an inexpensive place to live.

"All I knew was how to be a machinist," he said matter-of-factly. "So when Doc told me I'd never do that again I got pretty depressed. Some days I wished I was dead. A friend said I should come down here to the river to see the ducks. You know, to help pass the time."

He paused, lost in memories. "There weren't many ducks back then—maybe 10-15. I threw out bread and told them my troubles. It felt so good, I decided to do it again. I had nothin' better to do.

"They started looking forward to seeing me and I started looking forward to seeing them. You might say they saved my life. That's when I made a promise to bring food to them every day. I've been doin' it for two years now—rain or shine. Never missed a day."

"Why do you keep doing it?"

"They count on me," he said. "One time in the dead of winter I rescued two ducks caught in a chunk of frozen ice. Another time the ducks led me to their secret spot under the bridge where the water don't freeze in winter. I started leaving food there until spring so it wouldn't blow away."

"Have you ever considered quitting or asking someone else to do it?"

"Oh, sure. A while back, so many ducks was showing up I thought I'd have to break my promise. We was too poor to keep buying the food. The local reverend offered me money to pay for the grain if I'd keep doing it. But we was so poor I knew I'd be tempted to keep it. I told him if he could figure out a way to keep the food coming, I'd keep feeding the ducks."

"He spread the word," Duck Man continued. "The bank set up a Duck Fund where townsfolk could donate money for the feed corn. Then the local Piggly Wiggly decided to give me their stale bread. Now I can feed all the ducks, no matter how many come."

His grandson tugged at his sleeve. "Grandpa, tell her about the book. Make her sign the book."

"Don't worry, son. I'll get to it." The old man reached into the backseat and pulled out an inexpensive notebook.

"Once the word got out about the ducks and me," he said, "a couple newspaper reporters came down from Louisville. Then CNN came lookin' for me." He chuckled at the thought of CNN coming to Cadiz to interview a washed-up machinist.

The ducks honked loudly, shoving and nipping each other as if to say, "Cut the story, gramps. Keep the grub coming."

"People driving through Cadiz started looking for me, too. Imagine that! So I got this here book, so I'd know where they came from."

The tattered and stained book contained page after page of names and comments from people from all across the United States.

"This here couple was on their honeymoon," he said, pointing to an older entry. He flipped forward a few pages. "These folks had a carload of kids that wanted to tease the ducks. I set them straight in a hurry. 'Don't mess with my ducks,' I told them. 'They've got something to teach us.'"

"Like what?"

"Well, most folks I meet has got the 'hurry' sickness," he said. "They don't know where they're going, but they have to get there fast. But the ducks? They don't worry where they're going. All they care about is what's happening now. They don't even worry whether they'll have food tomorrow, because I gave them a promise and they know I won't let them down."

I swallowed hard and watched in silence as he continued to tenderly feed his beloved ducks.

Okay, God. I got the message.

Back in the car, I headed out of town, driving nowhere in particular. Just driving. Thinking about the fisherman and Duck Man, wisdom-bearers in plainclothes.

Meandering along some unnamed back road, a dilapidated, abandoned barn caught my eye. It set back off the road without any driveway leading to it. There were no other houses or barns as far as the eye could see. Its weathered gray siding and red roof reminded me of an Andrew Wyeth painting. Curious, I pulled off the road and drove slowly over the bumpy terrain to reach it, parking in a tall stand of grass out front.

A few rusty farm implements lay in the weeds next to the barn. Partially unhinged doors hung askew. Inside the barn, large sheaves of what looked like tobacco leaves hung upside down from the rafters. An old wooden stool set under the leaves, apparently for use when removing the tobacco bundles.

I pulled out my camera and leisurely worked the angles with the sun, enjoying the warmth of the sun and the anonymity of the setting. I didn't pay much attention to the surrounding area, except to note that a ravine and thick stand of trees concealed the barn to the outside world on three sides.

Inadvertently, I backed into an oil drum that lay on its side in a wooden sling. It appeared to be a makeshift cooker of some kind. Funnels and other implements nearby made me wonder if it was a "still" for making moonshine.

A low groan and heavy thud spun me around in a panic. A worn-out army boot lay on the ground in front of me. Directly above it in the barn's rafters, a mangy-looking mattress dangled out of the opening under the barn's eaves.

A bare human foot lay on the mattress, toes turned down. A rifle butt—barely perceptible in the shadows—lay on the floor of the rafters pointed outwards.

My heart beat like a jackhammer. I grabbed my camera bag and ran through the weeds to the front of the barn without looking back.

The car was locked—the automatic habit of a city girl—and I couldn't find my keys. I grabbed the spare set hidden under the left rear wheel, jumped in the car, and locked the doors. Grabbing the canister of pepper spray, I clutched the steering wheel to stop my body from shaking and gunned it for the gravel road.

I realized that "dropping out" may be what you do when you're having a midlife crisis, but it puts you at risk when you may need help.

I wish someone knew where I was.

Chapter 7

"What saves a man is to take
a step. Then another step."
 Antoine de Saint-Exupery`

LIFE IN THE REAR-VIEW MIRROR

I'm not sure why I threw my old journals in the trunk when I packed for the trip. Maybe I thought if I was going to figure out my future it might help to reflect on the past.

My last night at Lake Barkley I dumped the box of journals onto the bed, propped myself against a stack of pillows and settled in for a long read. I wasn't clear where to travel next. Maybe the journals would guide me.

I've kept journals for years. They're not great literature; the content is too raw. Sometimes the words more closely resemble a toxic waste dump than great prose. Still, they serve an important purpose. They're a safe place to deposit anger, confusion and disappointment, without fear of being judged or misunderstood. We can talk about our lives without blushing and siphon off the extremes of our feelings, without losing our minds.

Sweeping through several years of entries in one sitting was both eye-opening and depressing. The wide-angle view of my life provided just enough detail to prevent dismissal of the parts I wished weren't there.

I pulled out a yellow legal pad and began to jot down a timeline of the major events of my life—good and bad—and how I handled them. Did they change me? Do they still affect me today? Should they?

Around 2 a.m. I tossed the journals aside and stepped out onto the lakeside porch of my cabin to decompress. Staring at the moon's reflection off the lake, anger and tears swept over me in alternating currents as the night owls repeated their haunting night calls.

So many years spent trying to measure up, chasing somebody else's agenda for my life, making choices for all the wrong reasons. What a waste.

The next morning—for reasons I can't explain—I knew my next stop should be Nashville. I lived there as a child for three years. I remembered the address the way a young child remembers an address in case they get lost and has to repeat it to a stranger, but I wasn't sure I would recognize the house.

When an enormous magnolia tree came into view, I knew. I still have a snapshot in an old photo album of a chubby little girl in leather sandals and a Buster Brown haircut whose chief chore was to water the newly planted magnolia sapling in the front yard. It now shot 25 feet into the air, magnificent and awash in fragrant blossoms.

I pulled into the gravel driveway and rang the doorbell. A pleasant Black woman warmly greeted me.

"Sorry to bother you," I said, "but I lived in this house many years ago as a young child. I haven't been back since. I happened to be in the area and wondered if I might take a quick walk through the house for old time's sake? I know it's a bit bold to ask, but..."

She smiled warmly. "No, no, I don't mind at all! Come in! Come in! Excuse the mess. I haven't picked up around the house yet this morning."

She told me her family had lived in the house for more than 25 years. It had a comfortable lived-in look with afghans and family photos everywhere. Newly retired from an administrative post at a local university, she was awaiting the arrival of her fourth grandbaby.

After showing me around the main floor she asked if I wanted to see the upstairs. I politely declined. Nothing about the house registered as familiar.

It should have come as no surprise. I don't remember the interior of *any* home where I lived from the age of three or four until I became a teenager. It was a child's way of walling off hidden events that stole innocence and wounded the soul. Over the years, occasionally memories bled out of those walled-off pieces of my history. I had hoped that seeing the house might somehow settle some things. It didn't. The trail was cold. Pages of my story would remain missing or just fractured memories.

It's hard to understand a storyline if you start in the middle. I guess knowing more wouldn't have changed anything. Maybe it's time to stop looking backward for answers. The past wasn't pretty, but it's over. Trying to make sense of it decades later feels like a fool's errand. Time to move on.

The woman walked me to my car. After exchanging a few final pleasantries, I left. As I drove away, depression blanketed me like a dense fog. I felt agitated and unsettled. I just wanted to get away, anywhere, far away.

I headed east into downtown Nashville. It was the day of the annual Country Music Awards and—like Hollywood on the day of the Oscars—the city looked like a ghost town. Everyone must have been home getting ready to party.

Scouring the map, there weren't towns of any size south and east until you reached Chattanooga or Knoxville. But it looked like I could reach Fall Creek Falls State Park before dark. State park lodges had been a much better option than some of the crummy motels where I had stayed.

Hours later, heavy cloud cover hid the moon and stars, removing any sense of direction. I felt swallowed up in a black hole. Growing anxiety made my breathing shallow. None of the crisscrossing roads show up on the map and none of the roads had street signs. Something was wrong. My blinding headache didn't help.

*I should have reached the park two hours ago. I haven't seen a gas station or farmhouse or even another car for at least 45 minutes. Where **am** I? God, get me out of here! Send someone I can follow until I get my bearings!*

Almost instantly, two semi-trucks pulled onto the road. I couldn't even see the intersection in the pitch-blackness, but their headlights alerted me to their presence.

The gravel road seemed an odd place to find two 18-wheelers. There was no logical reason for them to be there. The area was completely devoid of commerce and they were far too big to easily maneuver the narrow roads that had no shoulder.

Nevertheless, they flanked me like a forward and rear guard. Slowly my breathing relaxed, the cramp in my shoulders loosened, and after several minutes our mini-caravan reached an identifiable intersection.

I dropped out of the convoy, honked my thanks, and made careful note of every turn until I reached the entrance to the state park. The lodge had one remaining room.

Thank you, God. Tonight my guardian angels were driving semis.

* * *

You don't need a visa to enter southern Appalachia, but a lexicon would help. Fortunately, the warmth and hospitality of the locals make up for any language barrier.

"How far to Mount Della?" I asked the owner of the gas station and mini-mart down the road from the state park.

"Aww, 'bout tain molls paste thuh nye-chur sin-tur." *

Clueless as to what he said, I pressed on. "Uh, do you carry any AA batteries?"

"Thuh bayet-trees arr rot uh-pair baaa thuh toe-eezz. Thing-cue fur bay-in suh pay-shunt." **

I stared at him blankly, still unable to decipher his dialect or extreme southern accent. (I couldn't tell which it was.) His wife pressed a cup of coffee into my hand, pulled up a rocker with a sagging seat, shooed off her husband, and grabbed my arm.

"Honey, come over here and sit a spell. Harold, get the poor lady what she needs before we both get too old to remember what she came for."

Harold pulled down some batteries and rang them up with the gas purchase as his wife launched into a long and animated monologue about a large poster on the wall behind the pork rind display.

It was a photograph of Fall Creek Falls, taken, she said, with her own point-and-shoot camera from K-Mart. She carefully explained that it cost $9.00 to order the picture in poster size from a mail order developer. She was selling it for $12.00 to any takers, after which she would order another one. Was I interested?

All this was ascertainable by watching where she pointed and catching semi-recognizable words every sentence or two.

I nodded intently to show I was paying attention and hoped I was not agreeing to something heinous. Her lone photograph was surrounded by several far more attractive photos of the same falls—pictures that were less expensive and far better quality, no doubt taken by professional photographers. The disparity was totally lost on her. It was, after all, *her* unique picture of the falls, which she was selling for the "bargain" price of $12.

* *"Oh, about 10 miles past the nature center."*
** *"The batteries are right up there by the toys. Thank you for being so patient."*

Her husband, an aspiring country music songwriter, picked up an old Gibson guitar and began interjecting his sales pitch at every opportunity in the conversation.

"Arrr yuh sure ya dunt know nubuddy in thuh recurd binness? I've writ some real purty songs." *

After enduring several more minutes of hard sell and after the complete depletion of my supply of small talk, I insisted I really did have to go. The wife patted me on my arm, put her arm in mine, and walked me over to the diner housed in the tiny cabin next door.

"The two grandmas who run the place see everybody who stops for gas, don't you know," she said in a whisper. "They tend to feel real bad if folks don't stop by."

The grandmas fussed over me as I feasted on turnip greens, pinto beans, cornbread, and sausage gravy. Still nodding and smiling an hour later, I backed out the screen door and made a dash to my car—securing my freedom with the purchase of a $1.25 piece of homemade wild blackberry cobbler.

*   *   *

Hiking around the state part later that afternoon, I had to admit the quirky gas station couple certainly didn't lack confidence and they seemed to have a clear picture of what they wanted in life, even if it wasn't deeply rooted in reality.

The wife fancied herself an accomplished nature photographer whose work deserved top dollar, even though the pictures were taken with a cheap box camera and she had no photographic training or experience or understanding of marketing.

Her husband, with his banged-up guitar, never doubted Nashville would someday come calling. His songs helped people

* *"Are you sure you don't know nobody in the record business. I've written some really pretty songs."*

understand life, he said. Isn't that the hallmark of every good country song? If country music legend Dolly Parton could come from the same humble beginnings and turn her outrageous dream into a successful music career, why not him?

Until that moment, I'd always felt that talk of having a personal vision for your life was like pompous corporate-speak. If you have goals, isn't that the same thing?

The purpose of vision is clearer to me now. It's what springs us out of bed in the morning and makes us excited about what's up ahead. It's our view of paradise, the place where we want to end up. And goals help us get there. Goals are servants of the vision— action steps to help make our vision a reality.

When there's no vision, goals flounder looking for someone or something to give them direction. Other people, friends, family, even our culture, are only too happy to fill the void—to foist on us their vision of what will make us happy.

Furthermore, if goals don't have any boss or a clear vision to guide them, they start acting like bullies—sitting out there in the distance, taunting our slow, uneven progress. They turn on us and produce guilt and insecurity, taunting us for our failures rather than helping us fulfill our dreams. Been there.

I think that's where our beliefs come in. If my beliefs are rooted in God's value system, they anchor my goals and vision and guide my behavior by what is timeless and eternal. I'm less likely to be swayed by the shifting winds of what's "in" and what someone else says ought to matter or ought to be worth throwing my life behind.

> **Vision**—a picture of my desired future, shaped by who I am, how God designed me, and what stirs my passion.

> **Goals**—to help me get there.

Clear Beliefs and Values—to anchor and shape my vision, goals, and behavior and help me make good choices along the way.

They all play a part. It also means any particular job or role or accomplishment is never the end game. They are just mile markers that are part of a bigger story written for my life. God planted the clues to any vision for my life by what makes our hearts sing—with the gifts and talents and passions planted in our DNA, which await our discovery and nurture. I had never really put it together coherently. Now it made more sense.

*   *   *

I headed back to the lodge to pick up my camera and get outside, to clear my head. The cleaning cart confirmed that the small woman sitting on the edge of my bed was the maid, but she looked like a child. She held in her hand the framed photo of my husband and me that I set out on the nightstand each night.

When I walked in, she jumped to her feet, embarrassed to be caught handling my things. She placed the picture back on the nightstand and started dusting and talking non-stop.

"Is that yur husband? You two sure are a sweet-lookin' couple. You got any kids? I got three—a boy, 16; a girl, 12 and another girl, 3."

She couldn't have weighed more than 90 pounds. She looked 16.

"I'm 31, but I got good genes from my momma. Folks think I'm a lot younger. I been working here seven years. I'm real proud of that. The State says if I stay for ten more years I can get a pension. Won't that be somethin'? Boy, howdy, I'd sure like to stop workin' then if I can. My momma worked two or three jobs at a time when we was growin' up. We didn't see her much. I love her though. She was just doin' what she had to do.

"Momma wants to retire when she's 55 so she can spend more time with her grandkids. Won't that be nice? It's kinda hard waiting for the time when Momma and me and the kids can be together. Hope nothin' happens in the meantime, if you know what I mean. Nothin' to mess up the plan. We been waitin' a long time."

Her voice trailed off. She had the saddest eyes I'd ever seen. I wondered if this fragile child/woman could hold things together until then.

I turned to leave. "Well, I just came by to pick up my camera. I'll leave you alone so you can work undisturbed. Thanks for telling me about your family."

"Y'all have a nice stay. This here's a nice place. You'll find lots of nice pichurs to take. I'll have everthin' all neat and purty for ya when ya get back."

I grabbed my camera and left.

*　　*　　*

According to the park sign, the view from the bluff extended 50 miles on a clear day. I could see North Carolina in the distance. Down below, a lush forested valley was coming alive with fall colors. Other placards at each overlook throughout the park commemorated people whose destinies ended there amidst the beauty—everyone from a famous climber who fell to his death off one ridge to a well-known botanist who died on one of the trails doing what he loved best, gathering plant specimens.

The world, it seems, is divided into two camps: those who do what they love now—regardless of the cost (like the intrepid naturalists and the gas station couple)—and those who hope to do it later (like the cabin maid). The happiest people seem to be those who don't wait.

Temporary dam work upstream had reduced the flow of Fall Creek Falls to less than show-stopping levels, but it was still impressive. As the tallest waterfall east of the Rockies, it plunged

256 feet into a shaded pool at the bottom of a snug canyon. It was definitely the crown jewel of the state park.

I arrived at the falls' overlook late in the day and planned to take photographic advantage of the longer shadows that come with the late afternoon light. Unfortunately, the position of the falls made morning light the best time of day for pictures. It meant returning the next day.

A handful of brave souls cavorted in the rocky pool below, their faint voices echoing off the canyon walls. It was hard to gauge how far away they were, since most of the trail that led to the bottom was hidden from view except at the beginning and end.

Four couples in trademark Amish garb bounded past me down the path. Impulsively, I took off down the trail behind them. The women were encumbered by their long flowing cotton dresses. I thought if they can do it, so can I.

The path was straightforward in the early going and then gradually steepened. Sandstone formations extended out over the narrow path, which wound back and forth along the canyon's rocky ledges into the forest. Large boulders lay strewn among fallen limbs and dense undergrowth.

As the path became more challenging I fell behind and lost sight of the Amish. I had never hiked any path more serious than a city forest preserve bike path.

I sat down to catch my breath and repositioned my camera around my neck so I could get down on all fours. Every step seemed a struggle as I tried to keep my footing, clinging to limbs, rocks, and anything that seemed secure.

Is this normal? I'm sure the Amish women didn't crawl around like this. Why haven't I met anyone coming back from the bottom of the falls?

The heavy foliage and the narrowness of the gorge brought darkness sooner to the lower canyon than to the top of the trail above me. I looked at my watch.

I'd better forget going the rest of the way. This is a lot more difficult than I expected. The ascent will be even harder. I'm in way over my head.

I turned around to look for the trail out. The path had vanished. A dense impenetrable wall of forest was all that remained.

*   *   *

"Helloooo! Can anyone hear me? Help! I'm lost!" My throat was soon raw from yelling for help. I wasn't sure how long it would hold out. The sound of the falls drowned out my voice.

I can't be lost. It's a public trail! I saw young families hiking it!

I kept climbing upwards, figuring eventually it had to lead me out. The steep incline forced much winding back and forth to gain even modest upward progress. Rocks kept crumbling underfoot and I struggled to avoid starting a rockslide that would fling me to the bottom of the canyon.

As darkness fell, the temperature dropped. Dressed in only a T-shirt and shorts, the cool evening winds gave me goose bumps, even though I was sweating from the climb. The sounds in the woods took on a more malevolent tone.

Someone is bound to hear me. I'm probably close to where I need to be but just can't see it. Stay calm and keep yelling.

The possibility of encountering a coyote or raccoon didn't scare me; I was ignorant of any danger they posed. Snakes were a different story. I'm terrified of snakes. I was pretty sure there were no bears in the park. This was not the Smoky Mountains. My cries for help became more urgent.

"Helloooo! Can anyone hear me? I need help!" After each shout, I waited for a response and then resumed my climb.

An hour later, a male voice echoed from above. "Hellooooo! Where are you?"

"Here! I'm down below you!"

Keep talking so I can hear where you are. Are you all right?"

"I will be when you get me out of here."

"I can't see you. Stay where you are and keep yelling. We'll follow your voice."

Ten minutes later two teenagers dressed in jeans and hiking boots reached me, scrambling the last 20 feet on their rear-ends. The redheaded young man with a military buzz haircut looked shocked.

"Ma'am, how did you get down *here*? You're way off the trail!"

"Oh…just a shameless ploy for attention," I said, feeling beyond stupid.

"Are you sure you're okay? You're shaking."

"I know. I'm freezing! I didn't exactly dress for getting lost. You have no idea how glad I am to see you. I was afraid I'd be stuck here overnight."

They gave each other a knowing glance. "Uh, that wouldn't have been such a good idea, Ma'am. The woods aren't…well…they aren't real friendly at night. That's why the park wants people off the trails before sunset."

"What trail!" I said in exasperation. "It just disappeared!"

"The trick is not to look at the ground. Look for the painted markers on the trees about six feet off the ground. There's too much shifting of rocks, leaves, and debris on the ground, so the Rangers mark the path on the trees—like the Indians used to do. Unfortunately, this late in the season the paint has peeled off in a lot of places. There are usually enough people on the trail to keep a person goin' in the right direction. Here, get behind me. Laura can bring up the rear. Just follow me."

"What were you guys doing down here?"

He turned around and gave me a wide grin. "Oh, me and Laura have a favorite spot we sneak off to now and then."

I suspected the attractive brunette was blushing but I didn't turn around to check. My legs were twitching from exhaustion. I hung close to him, crawling through the bushes until we were once again on what he assured me was the path.

When we got close enough to the rim of the canyon to see the top, I waved them on.

"I've got to sit down to catch my breath," I said, breathing heavily. "You go on without me. I'll be fine from here."

I looked them both in the eyes. "I am really, really grateful. I can't thank you enough." I shook hands with the young man and his girlfriend gave me a hug. They scurried up the slope and out of sight.

When I reached the top of the overlook, the parking area was empty except for my car. Off to one side of the trailhead I noticed a small, unobtrusive marker: "Moderately Difficult Trail."

Chapter 8

"If one advances confidently in the direction of his dreams and endeavors to live the life which he has imagined, he will meet with a success unexpected in common hours."

Henry David Thoreau
On Walden Pond

APPALACHIAN DREAMERS

A barrel-chested man in a black apron poured a bag of chunks into the boiling cauldron.

"What is that stuff?" I asked.

"Pork rinds—the best in Tennessee," he said. "Just watch these suckers puff up. Ain't they purty!"

"And cholesterol-free, right?" I said.

"Honey, if you're worried about cholesterol you cain't be from Tennessee." A wide grin spread over his face. "And you definitely ain't got no business comin' to The Homecoming."

He pressed the rinds down into the oil with a tool that looked like an oversized potato masher.

"Here. Try some." He reached for a small paper bag. "A whole bag for a buck, hot out of the kettle."

An older gentleman standing behind me leaned into our conversation. His belly protruded so far, I wondered what kept him from tipping over.

"Honey, all you gotta do is learn to flatfoot and you won't have to worry about no cholesterol."

"Flatfoot?"

"You know. Buck dancing, clogging. He pointed to two rows of clog dance championship pins that hung on his suspenders like Sunday school attendance pins.

"M' name's Bobby." He stuck out his hand. "Pleased to make your acquaintance. C'mon. We're about to perform. You can see for yourself."

I followed him through the crowd to a small wooden stage in one corner of the field. Men in bib overalls and straw hats played their hearts out on banjos, guitars, a bass, the fiddle, and washboard.

Dancers of all ages ran onstage in groups of six or eight and launched into high-energy footwork. After dancing in informal chorus lines, each person took a turn showing off their individual "show" steps, hooting and hollering the whole time. When Bobby jumped onstage he defied every law of physics, dancing like a wild man.

The photographer in Louisville was right. Doing something you love changes everything.

In other parts of the field, farm families sat under shade trees explaining to visitors about cream separators and barrel churns. Some sold ground cornmeal, wheat, and rye flour in small bags with recipes attached.

Mennonites from Muddy Pond, Tennessee, made molasses with the aid of a mule-drawn mill wheel. A blacksmith worked at a makeshift forge. Taxidermy and "tatting" demonstrations ran concurrently with lessons in how to make sassafras tea and mincemeat. It was like a hillbilly Woodstock, a chance for native Appalachians to explain themselves to the outside world.

Addled by sensory and sugar overload, I plopped down next to a log cabin on the edge of the field. A sign on the door identified it as the former home of Cordelia Peters Parks. Born there. Raised nine children there. Died there.

Two old-timers sat on the porch singing mountain tunes and strumming a banjo and guitar. Their wives accompanied them on tambourines.

"How long have you two been playing together?" I asked them between songs.

"Oh, as long as I can remember," one said. "We were raised in a family of 11 kids. Had no money for entertainment so we entertained each other."

"I joined the Army in '36," the other man said. "Little Brother followed me a couple years later. We started a country band in the service and that helped us stay together most of World War II and the Korean War."

They wouldn't reveal their ages but bragged they'd both been married more than 50 years. "Folks today sign up for their divorce when they pay for their marriage license. But me and Little Brother are in a contest to see who can stay married the longest!"

As if on cue, they launched into another medley of folk songs. Midway through the set, another man strolled over and joined in on his handmade mandolin. When the brothers took a break, I struck up a conversation with the man with the mandolin who stayed behind.

"Gentleman John" Irwin, it turned out, founded the festival. He had been a local school superintendent before buying the farm and turning it into a living history museum.

"That's a pretty drastic lifestyle change," I said. "It's not something you decide to do on a whim. What happened?"

He paused, weighing how much he wanted to share.

"The whole thing started years ago when I went to a local auction and saw a quilt made by the old Miller woman. City folks wanted to buy it and buy her butter churn, too, and turn the churn into a lamp. It seemed a shame—that quilt and churn ending up as nothing more than somebody's home decor. I thought the pieces were more important than that and should stay here—to tell the story of those who came ahead of us."

"What did you plan to do with them?"

"I didn't have a plan—at least not then. Years later, though, when I returned from the Army, I had another experience that helped me know what I needed to do."

"What happened?" I asked.

"Well, they were tearing down my grandparents' homestead and I saw them tossing out Grandma's nutmeg grinder." He leaned his head down and let out a long breath as if someone had sucker punched him. Thick bushy eyebrows hid his eyes from further disclosure.

"It sounds a little silly, talking about it now. But it really got to me—all those times I'd seen Grandma make custard and grate nutmeg on top of it. It didn't seem right to let those things go. It was the Miller woman's situation all over again." A long pause followed. "Then there was the quilt...."

"What quilt?" I asked.

"Well, Grandma was one of ten kids—always cooking and sewing and struggling to keep body and soul together. But every night after the chores were done she used to work on a Victorian crazy quilt. She loved that thing. When it was almost finished, she embroidered the words, 'Remember Me' in one corner."

His eyes filled with tears. "I vowed then and there that I would. I'd remember her. And I'd remember the old Miller woman, too. I'd make sure a lot of people remembered them."

We sat in silence as he looked around the field at all the activity and tried to compose himself.

"None of this is about the quilt or the butter churn, you know. It's about remembering."

I nodded in agreement.

"Did you know at the time how you wanted to remember them?

"No, I just kept doing the next thing," he said. "I kept accumulating things. Eventually, I bought an old log cabin to house it in, thinking other people might want to see the stuff, too.

"I laid a hose over the driveway and rigged it so it rang a bell when folks drove over the hose. We'd run out of the house and open the cabin and charge them 50 cents to cover our expenses. That first year more than 700 people came."

He described how other people caught the vision and wanted to donate their family's Appalachian memorabilia. He bought another log cabin. Then the farm came on the market.

His dream of honoring his ancestors and Appalachian culture began to take on a life of its own. The farm became the Museum of Appalachia—a living history museum open year-round to the public and to school groups and host of the four-day Tennessee Homecoming each October.

"Did you have any idea how big this would become?" I asked.

"Nope. I still can't believe it. I just put one foot in front of the other and here I am."

"That's quite a story," I said, not convinced it was that simple at all. "But I still don't understand how you could afford such a drastic switch from what you were doing?"

"Sometimes you do things because you ought to or because you can. There are other things you do because something pulls you toward it again and again. You have to do it, even if you're not sure why. If you don't act on it, you just know you'll end up with a mountain of regret."

After another long pause, he stood up to leave. "I have no regrets," he said. He turned and disappeared into the crowd.

* * *

Back in my motel room, I pulled out the timeline of my life that I had started a few days earlier in Kentucky.

*What themes or "pulls" have recurred in **my** life over the years? Did I pay attention to them?*

The biggest theme or pull that I could think of was just taking a series of progressively better jobs. But most of the time I took them for all the wrong reasons—the opportunity stroked my ego or offered more money, or I didn't have a good reason not to take it.

Later, when the fast track didn't "float my boat," I didn't understand why. Now I know. None of it was bad. It just wasn't the race I was born to run.

*   *   *

Driving for hours in a torrential downpour left me exhausted and cranky. To add to the misery, I hit the outskirts of Knoxville as 100,000 rowdy football fans poured out of Neyland Stadium. It was the annual big game between the Tennessee Vols and their archrival, the Arkansas Razorbacks. Traffic was gridlocked from one end of town to the other.

I pushed on to Gatlinburg but arrived too late in the day to cross the Smoky Mountains. Maneuvering the hairpin curves and switchbacks in a downpour and in the dark was not my idea of a good time, especially after what had happened on my way to Fall Creek Falls.

The foothills of the Smokies were breathtaking—picturesque winding creeks set against a backdrop of mountain peaks shrouded in mist and fog, exotic and mysterious. I wanted to stick around a bit and enjoy it. The rains had to take a break at some point.

The town of Gatlinburg is a garish tourist mecca of tacky attractions and souvenir shops all selling the same t-shirts, peanut brittle, and homemade fudge. Tour buses jammed downtown streets, offloading tourists in town for the "peak fall colors" weekend. Front desk clerks up and down the main drag dished out scorn for my failure to make an advance reservation.

"Madam, *surely* you're aware this is our most *important* weekend of the year." "Did you happen to notice the colorful trees?" (Insert disdain and ingratiating smile here.) "We have more than 100,000 motel rooms in the region, and I can assure you every one of them is booked. May I rent you a pillow and blanket for sleeping in your car?" (Insert an especially insincere smile.)

At my last best hope for a motel room, the clerk offered the room designated for handicapped patrons, at a rate 30% above the normal charge.

"That's the best I can do," he said, crossing his arms as if defying me to turn him down.

My body ached from fatigue. I was tired of the crowds of strangers everywhere, tired of fighting for a simple clean bed. My mind raced to frame remarks about what he could do with his room. In the end, the prospect of sleeping in my car bought my silence.

The rains stopped before dinner and I decided to take a brief walk along the creek behind the motel to clear my head and do a little dumping on God.

Okay, God, these repeated motel fiascos are getting to me. Are you rubbing my nose in the fact that I need to be more FLEXIBLE? Is this a not-so-subtle hint that I shouldn't contemplate a more unpredictable life if I can't handle disappointment?

Anger welled up.

Gimme me a break! I'm not used to this stuff! And, in case you haven't noticed, I am getting a little tired of trying to figure you out!

I began to hurl stones across the surface of the creek as my rant picked up steam.

I'm out here on the road trying to figure out what you want and what I'm supposed to do with the rest of my sorry life. I could use a little help here!

I feel like a rubber band that's been stretched to its limits one too many times. Crisis. Bounce back. Suck it up. Move on. Well, here's a bulletin! My 'bounce-back' is gone. Over. Done. Finis! Got that? I'm one crisis away from losing it completely!

Is that where you're headed with this? Break her down? Show her who's boss?

I picked up bigger rocks and targeted tree trunks on the other side of the creek with my rage.

*I'm tired of 'being strong', of 'handling' it! How about dishing out a little **normal** for a change? Do you have **normal** in your bag of tricks? And, while we're on the subject of normal, how about a normal **life**? You know, the two kids and the house in the suburbs? ...a manageable job without a psycho boss? ...no car crashes, no health crises, no divorce. Is that too much to ask?*

And another thing: What's up with the silent treatment? I'm hanging on by my fingernails, begging for a few lousy answers, and you've gone mute! In the Bible don't you say, 'Ask for what we need?' Well, I've asked... and asked... and asked! Are you listening?

My life feels like a giant jigsaw puzzle. You keep handing me more puzzle pieces as if I'll know what to do with them. But there's no PICTURE on the box! How am I supposed to put it all together without a PICTURE? What do you want from me, anyway? What's the point?

I fell silent, out of steam. Numbly I stared into the brook as the waters splashed over the rocks on their journey downstream.

The reply came swiftly. The words were as stunningly clear in my mind as if the speaker were sitting next to me in the flesh.

"I'm sorry you're in a hard place, Verla. I know what it feels like when the world is crashing in and it gets really hard.

"I do care about you. But I don't answer to you. That's not the way it works. And even if I gave you all the answers you're looking for, much of it still wouldn't make sense. I see things differently than you do and I see things you don't see.

"Besides, if I freely dispensed solutions without requiring any effort on your part, you'd never grow. You'd never develop the mental, emotional, and spiritual courage and muscle needed to handle what's coming later down the road.

"Real life isn't a fairy tale and this isn't heaven. Sorrow and pain are part of life on planet earth until I return to set things

right. I'm always near, closer than your breath, and I love you more than you can comprehend. Sometimes that will have to be enough."

My heart pounded like a jackhammer. My eyes were tightly shut and my head bowed, although I didn't recall assuming the position. I half expected some kind of Divine Hammer to fall on me as payback for my audacity and presumptuous whining, but the verbal 'dressing down' never came. Instead, it was as if a strong invisible arm wrapped itself around my shoulder.

"You don't need more answers, child. You need a deeper understanding of me. Then you'll realize I know what I'm doing and your life is safer with me than any of the alternatives— even when you don't have answers."

I began to weep. Some deep part of me knew he was right, but every fiber of my being wanted to prove him wrong.

"Not everyone gets assigned the same life," His words were firm but tender. *"You weren't created to be a middle-of-the-pack person who reaches a certain plateau and coasts the rest of the way. You were created to be a person who goes on ahead, scouts out the land, and comes back to help others find their way. But you have to find your own way first.*

"You do have a choice. You always have a choice. Do you want a life of your design or the one I intended for you? People who break new ground and fight for things that matter DO get beat up. That's the way it is. You can fight it or you can embrace it. If you accept it, I'll be with you every step of the way."

The words pressed in on me like a heavy hand. Then a strange deep calm settled over me, deeper than I've ever felt before or since.

"If you want me in charge, your life will often feel wild and untidy. But you'll also know what it means to feel alive. You'll soar with purpose and eventually you'll learn how to be content, regardless of your circumstances."

The words stopped. I sat in silence, not sure what to do next, oblivious to the fast-approaching darkness. I finally opened my eyes.

What just happened here? It feels like the most real thing that's ever happened to me, but if I ever have to explain it to someone they'll think I've lost my mind.

Emotionally drained, I walked back to my room, skipped dinner, and quickly fell into a deep sleep.

* * *

The rains returned and continued through the night. The next morning—still trying to sort out the experience by the creek—I took a leisurely scenic detour through the lowlands before tackling the mountain crossing.

Near Roaring Fork, out of curiosity I pulled onto an obscure dirt side road that ended almost as quickly as it began. There—directly in front of me—was a scene of such spectacular beauty I let out an involuntary gasp.

The woods sparkled in the morning sun with the rain's residue. Mossy rocks glistened in the sunlight that streamed down through the trees. It was the kind of illumination you see in movies just before an angel appears. Giant fern fronds sparkled with chains of pearl-like water beads. Blossoming ground cover draped the forest floor. The air smelled clean and fresh and a brook gurgled water as clear as fine-cut crystal.

I scrambled out of the car, grabbed my camera, and walked into the luminous glade as if drawn by an invisible magnet. Frantically I shot several pictures, praying I could capture 10% of what my eyes were seeing.

I never expect to see something like this again. It's Other Worldly. God, if this is a gift after last night's showdown, thank you. Really. Thank you.

* * *

The harrowing curves, steep grades, and intermittent fog made for a nerve-wracking mountain crossing. My neck and arms were so knotted, I could barely turn my head. Conditions didn't improve on the Carolina side, although the scenery along the high-altitude Blue Ridge Parkway was a visual feast. I pulled off the road onto an overlook to stretch my legs. Trees ablaze in gold, crimson, and burnished copper rustled just above a whisper in the valley below.

Tomorrow's my birthday—the first one I've ever celebrated alone. I'm a thousand miles from home and light years away from where I began, mentally, emotionally, physically, and spiritually. I didn't think I'd be gone this long. Is it time to go home? I've learned a lot, but I may never get the chance to do this again. I don't want to go home before the trip has fully accomplished its purpose.

Chapter 9

**"What you possess in the world will be
found on the day of your death to belong
to someone else, but what you are will be
yours forever."**

Henry Van Dyke

LIVES OF THE OTHER HALF

The most direct shot between Asheville and the Atlantic coast took me through the town where one of my husband's oldest friends lived. His friendship with Mark began when both were young hotshot lawyers in a high-profile Chicago law firm. Many years ago Mark had moved his family south to teach at a prominent university—an intentional career change to free up more time to indulge his passion for writing mystery novels.

There was much more to the story but I only knew part of it. It takes time to know another person's story and we don't usually make it a priority until we want to hear it for selfish reasons.

Time and circumstance had prevented me from ever meeting Mark and his family, but what little I knew about him intrigued me. How had he and his family actually done it—re-invented their lives? Did it work? Were they happy?

On a whim, I called him, introduced myself, and asked if I could drop by as I passed through the area.

Intuitively, George had already alerted them I was traveling through the area and might call. He had also told them it was my birthday. They insisted I plan to spend the night.

Their house blended into the woods like camouflage, tipped off only by the pine rockers and potted mums on the porch. A fox ran in front of the car as I drove in on a dense carpet of leaves.

We hit it off instantly. They whisked me off to a local Indian restaurant for dinner and extended the improvised birthday party back at the house—captured on tape by their precocious 10-year old, a budding videographer.

After their son went to bed, the three of us talked into the night about books and dreams and life's injustices, the politics of work, and the joys of friendship. As the logs burned down in their wood-burning stove, a chill fell over the house, finally sending us to bed in search of warmth.

After two weeks of the solitary life, it was exactly what I needed.

The need to connect must be written in our genetic code. Something happens in the company of others that doesn't happen when we're alone. We feel acknowledged, warmed and accompanied through life's gauntlet. Patience grows. Character is revealed. Selfishness is held in check and compassion gets its game on.

Little in life happens alone. Even the most basic of human rituals—birth and death—usually involve collaboration. In the absence of relationships, we're reduced to lesserlings.

I once read that famed artist Georgia O'Keefe felt relationships got in the way of her fulfilling her life purpose. So she lived most of the year in the Arizona desert in virtual isolation, insisting it helped her develop what she called keen eyes for desert colors. She went so far as to hire a hearing-impaired mute servant to handle the cooking and cleaning, to reduce any human interaction to a minimum.

She made it sound like excelling at what we're most gifted to do is somehow not possible along with life-giving relationships. They are too much work and too time-consuming. But God does his best work in relationships—both in us and through us. Jesus `demonstrated with His own life that the best way to live out a life calling is smack dab in the middle of messy, flawed, distracting relationships. That said, doing it O'Keefe's way sounds a whole lot easier.

* * *

During the relaxed evening of stimulating conversation with my hosts, I received several tips from their own experience for how to build a satisfying life when circumstances conspire against it.

Keep moving in the direction of your dreams. You can't redesign your life overnight. It takes time and a thousand small decisions made day in and day out.

Mark selected a new career that let him carve out blocks of writing time while still earning a living using his other skills. When he and his wife could afford it, they bought a cabin where they could take turns slipping away to write.

Let go of time wasters and energy leaks. Those who told us we could "have it all" failed to tell us hard choices would be necessary—financial choices, time choices, choices about what's "good enough." Their home reflected the lifestyle of people with more important things to do than keep an immaculate house. They abandoned certain notions of "normal" family life to make room for a lifestyle that supported their long-range game plan.

Do what you love because you love it—not because someone else says it's worth doing. Mark's first novel had not yet found a publisher but he was already at work on the next one, not waiting for permission to keep writing. His dream of becoming a published author was not unrealistic. He had talent and he was working hard at his craft, which increased the likelihood his vision could someday become a reality.

Act on what you know so far. Waiting for the planets to align with our plans will mean a very long wait. A better time may never come. Do the next thing. Believe that when you need further instructions they will be there.

*   *   *

When I left the next morning, a tropical storm was picking up steam along the eastern seaboard and heading north. My heart was set on going to Ocrakoke on North Carolina's Outer Banks, the desolate windswept peninsula off the coast that's known for its miniature wild ponies and sugar sand beaches. But the storm's path threatened to cut off access to Ocrakoke's one main road. I didn't want to drive all the way to the ocean only to be turned back.

Reluctantly, I turned south onto Interstate 95, which offered more options if the weather worsened.

By the time I reached Santee, South Carolina, fierce winds and heavy rain made it difficult to keep my car on the road. Radio stations an hour away in Charleston reported the opening of Red Cross shelters due to major flooding. Emergency preparedness officials urged motorists to stay out of the area.

I stopped at a restaurant near Lake Marion to decide whether to keep pushing south in an effort to bypass the storm. Men in fishing, hunting, and golf attire packed the dining room—driven indoors by the weather. The waitress welcomed them with a sunny southern drawl.

"I heard its raining farm animals out there, boys."

"It's a real frog strangler, honey. Time to do some serious 'nothin'."

Heeding their advice, I checked into a nearby motel and hunkered down to wait out the storm.

High winds and heavy rain pounded the motel as I curled up in bed to journal. I began to catalog how life on the road had changed my lifestyle in just a couple weeks.

My primary sources for news were now CNN Headline News (news anchors with big hair) and USA Today (which the locals called "McPaper"—a fast read, but not particularly filling).

My once-eclectic music taste had given way to country-music-all-the-time—not that there was much choice. Disc jockeys named Joe Bob, Rabbit, and Skeeter ruled the airwaves. I considered my Bubbafication complete when I could sing by heart every song on the "Top 10 Country Music Countdown."

Traveling on the cheap made healthy eating a challenge unless fast food and beef jerky are your definition of fine dining. Economy motels offered free breakfasts, but...define breakfast. Their offerings should have been dubbed Carb-O-Rama.

My token nod to healthy food was a protein shake and piece of fresh fruit for lunch, purchased on the run from gas stations or mini-marts.

By dinnertime, I abandoned all caution and indulged in regional specialties offered in local cafes.

In Kentucky, it was fried catfish, hush puppies, Burgoo and Derby pie. In Tennessee, it was cornbread, biscuits and sausage gravy with a side of turnip greens (or, as the locals called it, "Heart Attack on a Plate"). Brunswick Stew and Low Country Boil were staples in the Carolinas.

I was amazed by the behavior of fellow travelers. I watched families line up multiple ice chests and completely empty out motel ice machines before hitting the road again. Big dogs were smuggled into rooms and bath towels were smuggled out.

Motels responded with their own counter-measures. Fake headboards glued to the wall prevented furniture theft. Mattresses were placed on cheap wood frames instead of box springs. As one maid explained, "People don't steal mattresses if there's no box spring to go along with it."

Uh, how, exactly, do you check out of a motel with a mattress?

On the plus side, motels worked hard to accommodate repeat customers like over-the-road truckers. Since truckers often drive all night to avoid traffic, "Daysleeper" tags were hung on their doors to keep the housekeeping staff from waking them when they made their rounds.

Local residents along the way were relentlessly kind and hospitable. People went out of their way to offer detailed directions to anywhere you wanted to go, even if they had no clue how to get there. And they loved talking up their corner of the world.

"I'll bet you didn't know Kentucky ranks third behind Alaska and New Mexico for the most houses without indoor plumbing," one gas station attendant told me.

I'm not sure how I'll ever work that tidbit into a conversation, but his enthusiasm was infectious.

My car held up surprisingly well, except for the day the cruise control malfunctioned and I lurched from 65 MPH to 90 MPH in seconds without ever touching the accelerator. A terrifying ride on a short stretch of interstate. A local garage mechanic suggested with a deadpan face that I might want to avoid use of the cruise control until I could get it fixed. He reported that the manufacturer *had* issued a safety notice but no instructions were available yet for how to fix it.

I must admit life on the road had its appeal. Sleep when you want, eat when you want, never make a bed. No bills. No clogged plumbing. No responsibility. It may rot your character as a permanent lifestyle, but its attractions cannot be denied.

I'm more aware on the road of how I'm being shaped by my environment, positively and negatively. When I get home, I need to pay closer attention to the people, places, and experiences that I allow to shape me in that environment.

Nightly calls home anchored me to real life. George, Lisa, and I took turns missing each other. George joked about creating a hologram of me to keep him company at the dinner table.

Nevertheless, he repeatedly urged me not to come home until I was ready.

*　　*　　*

The storm delivered Charleston's worst flooding in 12 years and its worst weather since Hurricane Hugo six years earlier. As I hit the outskirts of Charleston, authorities officially closed the city to all but emergency vehicles.

Local military bases and all public schools were closed. Radio stations abandoned regular programming to recite long lists of the streets that were impassable. Dozens of cars stuck in ditches overtaxed the highway patrol.

I kept driving south in the opposite direction of the storm.

My change of plans opened up the possibility of attending a wedding on Hilton Head Island. A business acquaintance's daughter was getting married there. Before I left home she urged me to attend if I happened to end up in the area on that date—even if it turned out to be a last-minute decision and even if I had not RSVP'd. She would provide a complimentary room for me. I knew it would be a beautiful affair and I confess the chance to enjoy a decent hotel room after all my motel fiasco's was the clincher.

I assumed the dangerous weather had passed through Hilton Head by the time I arrived. But, to be on the safe side, I called the resort where the wedding was scheduled and asked about weather conditions.

"Everything's fine! Come ahead," the clerk reassured me with a bit too much enthusiasm. "It's business as usual."

*　　*　　*

I stared at the scene up ahead in disbelief. The road from the mainland to Hilton Head Island was gone. There was no *there* there! The swirling waters of the inter-coastal waterway had

91

engulfed the road and the water level was rising fast. Incredibly, cars continued to cross in both directions.

Drivers in the long line behind me laid on their horns, urging me to "get a move on" so we could all get across before High Tide hit in less than an hour.

Bowing to their pressure, I drove into the water, telling myself it must be safe if people were still crossing. I regretted the decision as soon as I hit the water.

Fear cemented my hands to the steering wheel as the car started to bob and float sideways. All efforts to steer failed.

A large car behind me began to tap my bumper repeatedly to keep me moving forward. I couldn't tell if the driver was a Good Samaritan trying to halt my sideways slide or if he was simply unable to control his own car as we both bobbed haphazardly across the fast-churning waters.

I was still trembling when I reached the island side and pulled into the parking lot of the island's Welcome Center. It was closed.

A handwritten note tacked on the door said employees fled the island to miss High Tide. The fact that tourism representatives wanted off the island didn't seem a good sign. I wanted to personally strangle the chirpy desk clerk who had told me to, "Come ahead!"

Most streets were underwater. There was no place to safely pull off the road because it was impossible to tell where the streets stopped and the sidewalk and grass began. Car traffic was virtually non-existent.

On one small stretch of barely-visible pavement I swerved to miss a baby alligator that slithered in front of my car.

*   *   *

After a hasty check-in, I grabbed my camera and headed for the beach a couple blocks away, hoping to stake out a safe sheltered perch from which to take pictures of High Tide.

The beach was a mess. The normally pristine shoreline was a long, narrow pile of sea debris as far as the eye could see.

Two middle-aged couples from Tiffin, Ohio, sat huddled together on beach chairs, drinking whisky highballs from a thermos and sharing cheese curls. All residents of their condominium had been ordered off the island. Since they were in no shape to drive, they opted to wait until morning to leave.

They toasted everyone from the National Weather Service to Jim Beam, coaxing the sandpipers to sip whiskey off a paper plate, then laughed as the birds staggered down the beach.

Their party was short-lived. Before we finished introductions and before I shot a single picture, High Tide smashed ashore with a vengeance, followed by pounding rain and frightening winds. Barely able to stay upright, I tucked my camera under my poncho and ran for the resort.

*   *   *

The next morning the phone in my room rang with a rude shrill. I rolled over and checked my watch: 5:30 a.m. Outside it was still raining hard.

"Did I wake you?" My husband's voice sounded unusually gentle.

"It's okay," I grunted, rubbing my eyes. "What's up?"

"I have sad news, honey. Irv's dead."

I shot upright in bed. **"What?"**

"He and Vonnie were at a conference," he continued. "Apparently, he got up in the middle of the night to go to the bathroom and had a heart attack. I'm so sorry. I know how much he meant to you."

I burst into tears. Irv and his wife had been close friends since I was 13. I dated his brother in high school. He had defended me once at great personal cost when someone wrongfully slandered me. Despite moves, job changes, children, and all the other things that short-circuit friendships, I never lost touch with them. I adored him.

"The funeral is tomorrow," George said. "I've already sent flowers."

"I…I don't know what to do," I said, trying hard to pull myself together mentally to formulate a plan. "I don't think I can make it back in time unless I drive all night."

"Honey, listen. I think you should keep going. I told Vonnie you were on the East Coast and it would be impossible for you to make the funeral. Lisa and I will go. Vonnie will be surrounded by a ton of family and friends. There's nothing for you to do unless you want to call or write her a personal note."

George waited out my tears.

"I don't know if staying on the road is the right thing to do," I said.

'Carpe Diem!' honey. Seize the day. Vonnie will understand. Really. Think about it before you try to come home. You know Irv would have said the same thing. It'll be okay."

*   *   *

Twenty-two inches of rain fell before the weather subsided. Once the waters began to recede and the roads became passable, I set out to explore the island to get my mind off Irv's death and to see the storm's aftermath.

Storm damage was significant but, strangely, there was still a palpable sense the island's rarified lifestyle remained safe and secure. Whatever was damaged would be repaired or replaced. This was, after all, Hilton Head, virtual reality for those who have the money to keep it that way.

Image rules on Hilton Head. The used car lot is not a used car lot. It's a "Cars of Special Interest" lot. There's probably an ordinance against having a bad hair day.

I've spent enough time around successful, wealthy people to know they're not that different from the rest of us except for the number of zeroes in their checkbooks. What bothers me is the self-absorption. Their ability to use their resources to buffer themselves from the world's unpleasantness often has a corroding effect on their capacity for empathy or compassion. Not always, but often enough to make me wary.

As a reporter I watched urban homeless people find shelter in cardboard boxes over street grates to gain control over *their* circumstances. I confess the way the wealthy on Hilton Head control their environment is considerably more attractive.

I learned an early lesson about the limits of wealth in my 20s. I learned it from a man who tried to teach me the exact opposite.

I was writing ad copy on spec for an ad agency he owned. The agency was not one of his more impressive holdings, but he loved to spend time there because he loved creative people. He, too, was creative—which made him a bit of an anomaly in traditional business circles. He felt the business world needed a lot more creative people. Maybe that's why he kept an eye out for them.

All I knew about his personal life were the stories about his infamous falling-out with his frugal billionaire father.

Traditional Dad still brown-bagged his lunch, while Flamboyant Son favored gourmet French restaurants and $150 bottles of wine. That was the least of their differences. Dad eventually told his son, "Go make your own fortune." Son did.

Son created a new product and then created a market for it, a very big market. When the money started rolling in, Son bought a vineyard in France, a golf resort in Florida, and a theatre in New York City, like the rest of us would buy Park Place and Boardwalk in a spirited game of Monopoly.

One day his secretary called to say my ad copy had come to his attention. He wanted to take me to lunch to find out what I wanted to do with my life. Days later, he picked me up in his Rolls Royce Corniche and I found myself sitting in a fancy French restaurant, eating escargot for the first time, listening to him rant about the ins and outs of success.

First, he said, you need to find a way to make a lot of money. "The first $100,000 is the hardest. After that, it's a simple matter of multiplication."

The point of making money, he said, was not to pile it up somewhere. Rather, it was to gain the freedom to do whatever you wanted. Whatever. You. Wanted. His picture of paradise was freedom—freedom from his Dad, freedom from convention, freedom from any kind of control.

He asked what I wanted. Not what kind of job I wanted or what kind of house I wanted to live in, but what did I *want*? What was my picture of paradise? He didn't call it vision, but I think his point was the same. It was the first time anyone had asked me. I didn't have a clue.

As I now reflected on his words years later on Hilton Head, I wondered why I still lacked vision when this man worked so hard to school me on its importance. Intuitively, I must have sensed that the values that underpinned *his* vision were not my values.

His values took him down a path of unfettered personal freedom and control over everything. It was a kind of Gospel According to Me. Without my realizing it at the time, that "eternity" gene planted in my heart the day I entered into a relationship with Christ wasn't buying that Gospel According to Me. Tantalizing? Yes. Satisfying? No, because I saw how his story ended.

His values did produce stunning results according to the prevailing sentiment of our culture. He was the embodiment of those success seminars that proclaim, "The sky's the limit!" "Control your own Destiny!" "YOU can make it happen!"

Sadly, after losing touch with him for several years, one day his secretary called me to report he was in the final throes of pancreatic cancer and wanted to thank me for our friendship and wish me every success. Despite his wealth and connections and his global search for a cure, his death sentence could not be postponed. He could not control his cancer.

I asked to see him one last time. His secretary said he didn't want to be seen in his weakened condition. He had no acquaintance with showing frailty and he was not about to change now.

I wrote him a letter to thank him for the time he invested in me years earlier and urged him to consider a different set of values than the ones on which he had built his life. It would mean admitting he needed help for what lay ahead. It would mean placing God in charge.

"What do you have to lose?" I argued. "You're running out of options."

A few days later I received his response, dictated to his secretary.

"Thanks for the suggestion," he wrote, "but it's too late to change course now. There's no room at God's table for a guy like me." He closed with words that still haunt me: "They don't tell you about this part in those success seminars."

I learned that wealth and success don't guarantee a happy ending and the wrong vision can be a dangerous thing if it's based on values that won't carry you across the finish line.

*　　*　　*

The pungent smell of southern barbeque pulled me off the road in front of a roadside fruit stand at the southern end of Hilton Head.

"Where's that smell coming from?" I asked the teenager behind the counter.

"It's Gideon's place out back," he grinned. "He's got a mess of chicken and ribs about to come off the fire. You should try 'em! But tell him I want a finder's fee for sending you."

I walked the short distance to find a tall Black man sweating over an open fire as he basted whole chickens and slabs of ribs with a dark thick sauce.

"How much?" I asked.

"…all depends," he answered, displaying a wide smile and prominent gold tooth. "How hungry are you? I've got four chickens and three slabs of ribs left. I'll make you a good deal if you want them all. Then I can go home early!"

"No, no! I can't eat more than half a slab. Are they fatty?"

"Fatty?" Gideon shrunk back in mock horror. "Honey, these ribs are so lean the pigs were shunned by their friends as an embarrassment to the breed. Say, do you want to take my picture? I can do a fancy flip with these ribs."

He picked up long tongs, turned away from the pit, and reached back over his shoulder in a contorted stretch. "I ought to be on TV I'm so good."

"No, thanks," I laughed. "Just the ribs. What comes with them?"

"They come with corn and baked beans—my momma's secret recipe. Mmmm. Maybe I should just close up and eat it all myself."

After another five minutes of his act, I paid for the somewhat pricey roadside meal and returned to my room with anticipation.

His act turned out to be better than his ribs, and his momma's name must have been Van Camp because the baked beans were ordinaire.' But he obviously loved what he was doing and he seemed a lot more real than the rest of Hilton Head.

* * *

The day of the wedding I couldn't get excited about any of the activities planned for the out-of-town wedding guests. The endless wet, gray days were getting to me and Irv's unexpected death made my trip and quest for a new life direction all the more urgent. I felt preoccupied. It wasn't time to party.

Mostly, I felt out of my league. Hilton Head was a place for Movers and Shakers and Beautiful People…not The Depressed and Insecure. I skipped all the festivities except the wedding and planned to make only a brief appearance at the reception.

The wedding was elegant and understated and the reception at the yacht club was first class in every way. The one dress I had packed for the trip was not exactly cocktail hour material, but it wasn't an embarrassment and no one knew me except the bride's parents, so it didn't matter. They understood it was a last-minute decision made while I was on the road.

Guests grazed at elaborate gourmet buffet tables and carving stations in several rooms that were all adorned with lavish flower arrangements. An excellent live band played in a spacious ballroom. It was a dream wedding. I lingered longer than expected.

Around 11 p.m. I walked out onto the marina's boardwalk and leaned against the railing, staring at the yachts, the harbor, and the starlit sky. Music, laughter, and the sound of tinkling glasses floated out into the night air.

If I return to the corporate world, this environment could someday be my life. But it's a tricky dance—trying to hold onto your values as the pace of the dance accelerates. Our lives are shaped as much by what we say "yes" to as those things to which we say "no." I begrudge no one who chooses this life, but I don't think this is the life I want.

Chapter 10

"Ob-fus-cate (ab-fe-skat) v.t. 1. to make
obscure, 2. to confuse or bewilder, 3. to
make unclear or indistinct."
Webster's Dictionary
Second Edition

ENGLISH ALLEGEDLY SPOKEN HERE

Both my Master Card and my license plates were due to expire at the end of the month. The new card and license plate renewal sticker arrived back home while I was traveling. Once I knew I would be on Hilton Head at least a couple days, I asked George to rush them to me. Three days later when I was ready to leave the island they still hadn't arrived.

The front desk clerk suggested I check with the local post office, vaguely hinting the letter might have been returned if it was sent to the resort's street address instead of its post office box.

*   *   *

"Yes, ma'am. May I help you?" The postal clerk flashed his most winsome Hilton Head Happy Face.

"I'm looking for a letter that should have arrived by now," I said. "I'm about to leave the island. Would you please check to see if it's here?" I handed him a slip of paper with the address I had given to George.

"Oh, that's too bad," he said, looking at the address. "It was probably returned." He returned the slip of paper to me, his smile unchanged. "Is there anything else I can help you with?"

"Wait," I said. "Returned? Why would it be returned? This is the correct address for the resort, isn't it?"

"Yes, ma'am. We just don't deliver there."

"Why not?"

"Because they don't have a curbside mailbox. They have a post office box here at the post office."

"Then why wouldn't my letter just go into their post office box?"

"Because it was addressed to their street address. We don't look up box numbers."

I stared at him, speechless. "It's a small island. It's probably the biggest resort on the island. It's been there for decades. Don't most postal workers know the box number?

"Yes, ma'am. We know it well. We just don't put mail in their box unless it's addressed to their box number."

"Well, if you can't drop it in their mailbox, wouldn't your carrier drop it off at their front desk when he's dropping off packages on his daily rounds?"

"Ma'am, most people on the island only live here part of the year. We don't know when they're here and when they're not. They don't want us delivering mail to their door when they're not there."

I interrupted him. "THE RESORT DOESN'T LEAVE! IT'S HERE ALL YEAR! I'M SURE THEY WOULD NOT BE OFFENDED IF YOU DELIVERED IT TO THEM!"

"Yes, but they don't have a curbside mailbox."

My head hurt.

I leaned over the counter to get as close to his face as possible and said very quietly, "How about checking in the back— wherever it is you put things that don't have a place to go—to see if my letter might be there? Could you do that for me? You check. I'll wait. If it's not there, I'll go away. I promise."

He trotted off, his smile still intact, and returned a few minutes later with my letter.

*   *   *

I spread out a map of the southeastern states to chart my next move. I really wanted to backtrack to Charleston and Ocrakoke, but the risk of running into more bad weather convinced me to keep traveling south. Colder weather was coming. A route that followed the sun made more sense.

New Plan B: Go as far south as Jacksonville, Florida, then turn west along the gulf coast toward New Orleans. Next stop: Savannah, Georgia.

*   *   *

History demands an audience in Savannah. Every block has a story to tell. General Jackson lived *here*. The Confederate Army was headquartered over *there*. Author Flannery O'Connor grew up in *that* little house, sandwiched between those Victorian mansions.

As American novelist William Faulkner once said, "The past isn't dead in the South. It isn't even past."

Savannah was smaller than expected, dotted with majestic antebellum homes, fountains, gas street lamps, statues of historic figures, and endless cypress trees dripping exotic gray moss.

Factor's Walk, the warehouse district that originally housed the Cotton Exchange, U. S. Customs House, and other historic landmarks, now housed a mix of trendy specialty shops. The smell of fresh-baked pralines lured me off the cobble-stoned street into a candy store.

The woman behind the counter scooped a chunk of the pralines onto a cleaver and passed it across the counter for me to sample.

"You're from up north, aren't you?" she said.

"How'd you know?"

"You're wearing shorts and a t-shirt—like you're trying to fool Mother Nature into thinking it's not October. Everyone here is wearing dark slacks and sweaters by now, except for the snowbirds passing through on their way to Florida. They always wear white. It's their uniform."

"But it's 75 degrees! It's too hot for sweaters!

"We Southerners like to pretend we're changing seasons," she said, "Frankly, I'd like to forget this one. It's like monsoon season!"

"No kidding! I just left Hilton Head. It's a mess there. But this area doesn't look that bad."

"Oh, honey, we got 14 inches of rain in 24 hours! More than 700 homes flooded in Chatham County alone. We're now an official federal disaster area, along with Charleston. Go check out Tybee Island. It's pitiful."

She was right. The beaches on Tybee Island were completely decimated. Despite a recent $7 million dollar oceanfront restoration project—the third one in recent years—all that remained of the six miles of shoreline were mounds of ocean garbage.

*　　*　　*

The six Asian businessmen who sat near my table spoke little English. The waitress approached them and, in her best Southern drawl, launched into the daily specials, along with a lengthy explanation of the restaurant's famous fried chicken and its special preparation.

An animated discussion between the visitors ensued in their native tongue, after which one of them said meekly, "You repeat, please?" She began again from the top, sparing no details. More furrowed brows and group-talk followed, along with a frantic search through their English/Japanese dictionary.

Finally, the exasperated waitress came over to my table.

"Honey, can you come over here and repeat what I'm saying, we'll be here all night. You'd think I was the one speaking a foreign language!" I tried not to smile, since I, too, could barely understand her drawl. Between the two of us, the businessmen eventually settled on their selections.

When the food arrived the gentlemen stood in unison, turned toward my table, and bowed profusely, speaking what I can only assume were words of gratitude. Later, as they were leaving, each man came to my table and bowed again, shaking my hand enthusiastically.

The waitress showed up behind them with coffee for me.

"Forgive me for not bowing, honey. I don't even curtsey for the Queen. The coffee's on me."

*   *   *

A billboard praising the beauty of the Georgia shore persuaded me to make a quick detour to Jekyll Island. It was a ghost town. Like Virginia Beach further north, the island's "season" was over and most attractions were closed. Its desolation only further fueled my melancholy. I made a final swing through Millionaire's Row, the island's historic district that was once the summer compound of wealthy tycoons like the Rockefellers, the J.P. Morgans, and the Pulitzers.

Life on the road is entertaining and it massages my discontent. But strangers and empty streets aren't much help in dealing with grief and loneliness.

*   *   *

It was well after dark when I reached the Okefenokee Swamp near Waycross, Georgia. The area reminded me of those southern rural towns portrayed in movies where strangers disappear without a trace. I picked the first motel off the main road to get safely settled in for the night.

A trucker hauling new cars to a Florida dealership came in behind me to register. The desk clerk made a special point to tell both of us...twice...that police patrolled the parking lot regularly. It only heightened my anxiety.

The trucker moved his rig under the brightest lights in the parking lot as an extra precaution. I followed suit. Cops or no cops, I wished it were morning. I feel safer in big cities. I understand cities. Here I felt like an escapee on the lam—even if my escape was not from the law but from my well-ordered life.

George had been anxiously awaiting my nightly call. His brother had been fighting a brain tumor for a long time in a New England nursing home. He had taken a turn for the worse and was now in a coma. Doctors asked George to consider decisions that would almost certainly hasten his brother's death. He was inconsolable.

He asked me to route myself north instead of west along the Gulf Coast. Then, if or when it became necessary, I could leave my car somewhere and fly to join him at his brother's bedside. Later, depending on what happened, he would fly back with me to where my car was located and together we would drive home.

After we hung up, I threw myself onto the bed and burst into tears. It was one sadness too many.

All the driving, the aggravations, the expense of the trip, and now this. It looked like another death might be imminent. I wrestled with whether the trip had been worth the high price of not being available to those I love when it matters most.

I hate it when decisions aren't black and white but action is required anyway.

* * *

The north end of the Okefenokee Swamp was wilder and less attractive than better-known parts of the swamp like Cypress Gardens further south. Nevertheless, as long as I was there, I opted for a boat tour through the swamp's dark passages.

While waiting for the next boat, I chatted with a docent who walked the pier carrying a small alligator in his arms.

"Family pet?" I said. "Or are you helping him scout out lunch?"

"You're safe." The young man smiled. "They're not like crocodiles. Alligators are afraid of humans. They only approach when tourists throw them food."

"What's a person supposed to do if that happens? Turn tail and run?"

"You can't outrun them. They can run 35 miles an hour. But if you run in a zigzag pattern, you'll be fine. They don't know what to do."

"And if I fall in the swamp?"

He laughed. "The alligators have gone into hibernation for the season, so you're safe. They're not interested in food. Besides, the swamp's only four or five feet deep, so you could literally walk back onto land."

A dockhand helped me onto a small flat-bottom boat already occupied by nine wisecracking farmers from Tuscaloosa, Alabama. They wore matching black caps with an eagle and the letters ALFA (Alabama Farmers Association) embroidered on each one.

The addition of a woman to the group sent their silliness into overdrive. They insisted the bird on their cap was a turkey buzzard, Alabama's new official state bird.

As we pulled away from the dock our tour guide pointed out an enormous 90-year-old bull alligator named Oscar, asleep on the riverbank. Oscar, we were told, was quite the ladies man with a reputation for bedding all the female alligators in the swamp.

"...just like Big John sitting next to that purty lady," one of the farmers retorted. "But don't you worry, honey. We'll protect you." Howls of laughter.

"I feel better already," I said.

"Don't listen to him," Big John grinned, poking his buddy in the side. "This is the guy who makes his wife bale hay while he sits in his truck supervisin'. Big protection he'll be."

"Well, I've got to keep an eye on her. Cain't let her go to town," his buddy answered.

"Why not?" I asked.

"She'll be ruin't, gettin' all those Big City ideas."

"Uh, oh," I said. "Then I'm in trouble. I'm from the Big City."

They gasped in mock horror as one farmer leaned forward with a squinty look.

"Say, you ain't one of them women's libbers, are you?"

"Gosh, I don't know," I teased. "What do they look like?"

"Aw, you know...like some kind of he-she." More howls.

The fellow sitting next to him nudged him in the ribs. "Virgil, that's prejudice, plain and simple. This poor girl's gonna think you really believe that hog mush."

"Hell, I cain't hate coloreds no more. Who am I gonna hate?"

Another farmer interrupted. "Honey, ignore him." He gave his friend a beady stare. "If he don't cut it out, in about a minute I'm going to wring his ugly red neck. Hand me a cig, you old fart, and put a cork in that big mouth of yours."

As the farmers continued their banter the tour guide continued his spiel while maneuvering us through the murky waters. The swamp was so dark and brooding, taking pictures was pointless.

The conversation fell into a comfortable cadence with no one revealing very much. By the time the boat docked again back at the pier, the farmers invited me to stop in and see them if I ever made it to Tuscaloosa.

We all knew that would never happen, in the same way I knew Virgil did not make his wife put up hay and Big John probably never bedded anyone but his childhood sweetheart who had been his wife for 45 years.

They were just trying to make their plain lives more exciting, while I was trying to make mine more sane. Everyone wants to be someone they're not.

Later, driving north, ironically, through a town called Enigma, Georgia, I realized I hadn't taken a single picture of the fun-loving farmers. It didn't matter. A picture wouldn't tell me who they really were. I don't think they wanted me to know.

.

Chapter 11

**"I had to scratch an itch. I didn't quite
know what the stakes were or what I
was heading for. Sometimes you don't
know what the agenda is. I just knew
that something was wrong."**

> *Ffyona Campbell, who*
> *took 11 years to walk*
> *around the world*

CHOICES

Everything changed after Hilton Head. The shock of Irv's death
and my brother-in-law's fight for life threw me onto autopilot. The
light-hearted Alabama farmers broke my malaise only briefly.

Life took on a dull sameness. Take pictures. Observe people.
Write down insights. Move on. I felt like a researcher at the
Library of Congress—cataloguing information that might be useful
someday to someone but which didn't matter much at the moment.

The farmers had urged me on my way north to stop at
Amicalola Falls at the southern tip of The Appalachian Trail. The
falls weren't the main attraction, they said. Rather, it was the view
from the state park lodge high atop Springer Mountain.

I pointed myself in that direction and started driving.

I was the lead car in a long line of cars on the crowded highway,
when the blinding glint of something shiny snapped me to
attention. We were all moving along at a pretty good clip.
Suddenly a flatbed truck flew past me traveling at least 85 miles an
hour. The truck veered sharply in front of me from the passing lane
to move to the head of the line.

His reckless maneuver caused his oversized load of long steel rods to reshuffle. One 10-foot-long rod from the top of the pile began to shimmy out of the bundle, bouncing closer to my car with each bump in the road.

I laid on my horn to warn the driver his load was coming apart. He thought I was simply angry over being cut off. In a fit of rage he hit his brakes to curtail his speed, forcing all of us to follow suit to avert a multi-car pileup.

Drivers behind me immediately pulled into the passing lane to get ahead of the hotheaded trucker, but when anyone tried to pass him he sped up, leaving them vulnerable to oncoming traffic and forcing them back in line.

It was war. Nobody in front or behind gave an inch and I was pinned in the middle. We were traveling nearly bumper-to-bumper at 80 MPH while the loose steel rod from the flatbed inched its way closer and closer to my windshield.

Without warning, the trucker accelerated as quickly as he had cut his speed minutes earlier. As the truck lunged forward, the loose rod zoomed toward me like a missile.

I threw up one hand to shield my face and ducked forward into the steering wheel, trying to keep one eye on the road. The truck's acceleration created a small open space between our vehicles. Incredibly, the front end of the rod hurled into the pavement in front of me like a javelin, missing my car by inches before it bounced into the air again and flipped into the ditch.

I screamed and began to shake, unnerved by the close call.

Up ahead two other cars chased down the truck to wave it over before its load further unraveled. Another driver passing on my left gave me a thumbs up and mouthed, "Are you alright?" as we both sped down the road trying not to get rear-ended by the heavy traffic behind us—all of whom were oblivious to the close call.

I held my hand over my mouth, shaking my head in disbelief. At the next exit I pulled off the highway and sat in my car, still trembling, forcing myself to take deep breaths to stop the panic.

Oh, God. You've felt so distant, but you were paying attention when it mattered most. Thank you for protecting me. Thank you from the bottom of my heart.

* * *

The steel rod incident and 400 miles of driving left me completely wiped out by the time I reached Canton, Georgia. I wasn't sure I could make it all the way to Amicalola Falls before stopping for the night. Canton's only motel (20 rooms) was completely booked.

"Can you recommend another motel in the area?" I asked the night clerk.

"Nope."

"How come?"

"…aren't any."

"Why not?"

"Nothing to do around here. No museums. No tourist attractions. Nobody comes here."

"Then why are you full tonight?"

"Don't know."

"Where's the nearest motel?"

"Atlanta."

"Atlanta! That's 40 miles back! How far is it to Amicalola Falls?"

"About 26 miles."

"Is that all? Then I'll just keep driving and stay at the lodge."

"Have you been there before?"

"No."

"You might not want to go there tonight."

"How come?"

"It's dark."

"I know, but it's closer than Atlanta. I don't want to backtrack."

"Nobody goes up the mountain at night."

"Why? Is it dangerous?"

"Nope. It's dark."

Frustrated, I walked out, found the nearest pay phone, and called the lodge to reserve a room. I told them to expect me within the hour and, after a hasty meal at a local café, I took off for the mountain.

Driving along the mountain's desolate winding roads under a pitch-black sky felt like Fall Creek Falls all over again, except the ascent was steeper. A misty drizzle began to fall. I hadn't seen a single car since leaving Canton.

A road sign appeared, warning that the last mile and a half to the lodge was a steep 25% grade ascent. Almost immediately the road angled upward so severely I felt like an astronaut lying on my back in a space ship. The darkness and rain exaggerated the incline. After what seemed like an interminable ascent, the lodge at the top of the mountain came into view. I let out a full-throated yell of relief.

*   *   *

The next morning I dressed quickly to make it down to the dining room before they stopped serving breakfast. To air out my room, I flung back the drapes to open the window. The view stopped me in my tracks.

More than 2,700 feet down below, the valley was an electrifying blaze of red, gold, orange, and copper-leafed trees interrupted only by wispy fog that snaked through the lower altitudes. It was the most spectacular display of fall colors I had ever seen.

Downstairs, the lobby was more like an oversized family room—decorated with roaring fireplaces, overstuffed sofas, pine rockers, and handmade quilts. A wall of glass gave visitors another unobstructed view of the breathtaking valley below.

After breakfast I settled in by the fire to journal and watch the passing scene. A group of seniors from a local Baptist church dropped in for an early lunch. Georgia state judges broke from their continuing education meetings to stretch their legs and take in the grandeur.

Later, when outside temperatures rose, I moved to a rocker on the veranda to people-watch. The reaction of guests was always the same. They would stroll outside chatting with companions, then stop conversations in mid-sentence when they saw the view. Nature commanded their attention without uttering a word.

*   *   *

The accent of the couple standing next to me at the top of Amicalola Falls suggested they might be from New York or some place where asphalt and high-rises were more the norm than scenic vistas.

The mom kept a close eye on her two boys as they edged close to the falls.

"Wow! This is awesome!" The younger boy was enthralled.

"How'd you like to be a drink of water going over those rocks," his older brother chimed in. They threw pebbles over the side and watched them sail 729 feet to the bottom.

Dad, an overbearing presence in impeccably tailored silk shirt and slacks, interrupted them.

"OK, I've got the falls." He shut off his fancy camcorder and began to pace. "Anything else to see up here?" he said to his wife.

"The lodge," his wife said. "It's all glass on one side. You want to take a look?"

"Naw, I just want scenery. Let's go."

"But, Mitch, we just got here! The kids haven't had a chance to look around and we haven't seen the falls from down below!"

"What's to see? We've got it on tape. We'll watch it when we get home. We've got to go. We've got three more places to hit before dinner."

He dashed for the car and shot out of their parking space without ever turning to see if his family was following him. The boys and their mother exchanged knowing looks, then hurried to catch up before dad left without them.

Watching this on a TV screen is better than enjoying it in person? Mitch, get a life!

Almost immediately, I felt guilty for being so quick to judge the man.

Aren't you the person who has measured every moment of this trip by whether it had a point and offered answers to your questions? How about if you enjoy the moment? This trip is an open-ended opportunity to indulge your curiosity. The answers will find you when it's time.

*   *   *

Someone forgot to tell the proprietors of the dilapidated grocery store/gas station/general store deep in Appalachia that it was no longer 1954. The cans and packaged foods on the shelves bore brand names I'd never heard of: Made-Rite sandwich spread, Blue Plate mayonnaise, pancake mix with a politically incorrect slave-style picture of Aunt Jemima.

None of the food items carried expiration dates or ingredient labeling and there was no rhyme or reason to how the merchandise was organized. Feminine products shared shelf space with cake mixes, fan belts, and fresh tomatoes. Used hunting boots were stacked next to Sarsaparilla.

The point of my stop was to buy lunch. But after scanning the shelves I wasn't sure my stomach was up to the challenge.

Pickled eggs and a wheel of aged cheddar lay uncovered on the counter for anyone to handle, including the man in a smelly sweatshirt, ragged jeans, and army boots who was manhandling the cheese. He flicked his cigarette ashes on the cement floor as he explained he'd just come from hunting wild boar and coyotes south of there.

Two men in camouflage gear came in to buy six-packs and propane gas. They sat down on wooden crates around a space heater to have a smoke and a chat with the proprietor.

A gaunt one-armed woman behind the cash register turned out to be the proprietor's wife. She talked non-stop about how she wished someone would take over the store so she and her husband could retire. As she spoke, she waved her bent arthritic index finger at everyone in the place, leaving the impression we were all in trouble for doing something really, really bad.

A Rottweiler named Frisky roamed the store at will. The woman said he wandered into the store from the woods two years ago and never left. That launched her into another story about Curly, their 18-year-old "real" dog that she insisted the vet killed.

"They must have been experimentin' on 'im. Poor thing. I know'd he'd of lived a while longer. He knew I needed him. Cost me $511 and all I got back was a dead dog. Don't that beat all? Good watchdog, he was."

I paid for my modest purchase—a frozen ice cream sandwich and a Coke in a tiny old-fashioned green bottle—and wished her well. Once outside I fed the ice cream sandwich to Frisky, who tried hard to jump into the car and leave with me. Apparently he, too, was looking for a way out of Dawsonville.

*   *   *

By Day Three on the mountain the fog was so dense I felt suspended in a bubble. Arriving guests hoping to catch the last of the fall colors might as well have scheduled a weekend trip to a closet.

I checked out and drove to the Visitor's Center near the foot of the falls, hoping the fog would lift before I had to make the steep descent down the mountain.

The Visitor's Center was the southernmost tip of the 2,160-mile long Appalachian Trail, the world's longest marked footpath. The TV monitor at the Center was playing a PBS documentary about seven friends who had hiked the entire length of the Trail and videotaped their experience. The video was playing to an empty room. I sat down to watch.

Their journey began on Springer Mountain not far from where I was sitting. It ended 4-1/2 months later on Mount Katahdin in northern Maine.

Several minutes into the video a young man in serious hiking gear sat down beside me in front of the television. He shed his enormous backpack and focused intently on the screen. He smelled like someone who hadn't showered in at least a week.

"Pretty gutsy group," I said quietly, once the video ended and the tape began to rewind.

No response. The young man continued to stare at the now-black screen.

"Have you been out on the trail?" I pressed.

"Yeah." He turned to look at me. His eyes were gentle—the color of blue marbles—but the rest of his body language announced wariness.

"Have you walked the whole trail?" I asked.

"Almost." He turned back toward the darkened screen and stared straight ahead.

"How long were you out there?"

"Long enough."

"You probably have great stories to tell."

"Yeah."

"Why are you doing it?"

"Because I want to."

"Isn't it dangerous hiking alone?"

"Yup."

My mind searched for a question that would require more than a one-syllable response.

"That kind of challenge is foreign to me," I said. "I can't stand giving up a hot bath, much less the other challenges of such a trip. Pretty pathetic, eh?"

"You get used to it."

"Were you trying to prove something?"

"No."

I pressed on like a Chatty Cathy doll, hoping to get him to open up. I couldn't figure out why he sat down right next to me in a huge room of empty chairs if he didn't want to talk.

"I admire your guts," I went on. "I'm not good at taking risks—not even with things I feel passionate about."

He turned and looked at me with a penetrating gaze. "Who are you?"

"Excuse me?" I backpedaled, realizing I had definitely crossed a line. "You mean, what's my name? Hey, I'm sorry. Too many questions. I have this annoying curiosity about everything. Really, I didn't mean to..."

"No, I mean, who *are* you?" He paused. "I'm a mountain climber. Who are you?" He didn't ask in disgust. His tone was kind—as if he wanted to help me find whatever I was working so hard to figure out.'

I gave him a blank look. "Well, I...uh...well...I'm a writer, I guess." The words came out in little more than a whisper.

"That's all you need to know," he said. "Start there." He turned back toward the TV monitor and resumed his penetrating stare as the TV replayed the documentary.

For several minutes I sat in silence, not quite sure why his question took me aback.

All those words from the biker in Seymour, the photographer in Louisville, the preacher in Cadiz, Gentleman John Irwin at The Homecoming and all the others...figuring out what makes their hearts sing and doing something with it, without obsessing about a title, a venue, the pay scale, the career path, or whether it was significant. It's about being who you are, they all said— doing it well, doing it some more, persevering even when it's hard. The joy will follow.

I've been insisting it had to look a certain way or be applauded by certain people. Trying to make it fit everyone else's expectations, when it was so obvious all along.

An elderly couple stepped through the doorway of the Visitor's Center and spotted the hiker, shouting to him from across the room. He broke into a wide smile and stood up to collect his backpack. They rushed over and wrapped him in a warm embrace.

"Look at you!" the old man said with joy he could barely contain. "Aren't you a sight for sore eyes. We've been a little concerned for you, boy, bein' several days late and all."

"I'm fine." He smiled broadly and gave the old man's arm a reassuring squeeze. "I'm really glad to see you." His voice betrayed his exhaustion.

Without a word, he followed them out the door. In an instant, they were gone.

I envied the hiker's clarity—a loner who tackled the Trail just because it was inextricably linked to who he was. His personality, passion, athleticism, and dreams all coincided to put him on the Trail. He needed no permission. He owed no one an explanation. He made no excuses and had no regrets. He hinted there had been a price for living on such uncomplicated terms. But there was a joyous freedom and resolve that was palpable. I wanted that.

I turned back to the TV documentary which had resumed onscreen. The one female in the group of hikers was asked what it felt like to reach the summit of Mt. Katahdin, Maine, at the end of the Trail. Reaching the summit, she said, was never the point. It was all about the journey.

*　　*　　*

I almost missed the tiny roadside stand until I caught the strong smell of boiling peanuts. A crude cardboard sign propped up against a stump read: "Boiled peanuts, $2 a bag." An old man stood over a metal drum filled with boiling salt water and raw peanuts.

"I guess I can't leave the Peanut State without trying some boiled peanuts," I said.

"Reckon so."

"Do you live around here?"

"Yup...just down the road. Lived here all my life."

I handed him two dollars.

"That's quite a kettle you've rigged up."

"My son made it for me. He's 38. He works for the railroad. He also made me this here scoop." The bottom had been cut off a tin cup and replaced with wire mesh. The cup was welded onto a makeshift pole—a perfect ladle for removing the peanuts from the deep drum.

"Where do you get the peanuts?"

"I grow 'em on my farm."

"Is this how you sell your peanuts?"

"Yup. Most peanut farmers sell their crop to the big food companies, but I don't raise enough for 'em to want mine."

He drained a ladle of peanuts and poured them into a waxed bag, then gave me a smaller sack for the shells.

"Watch out for the steam comin' out the top. It'll scald you right good."

Mason jars of vegetables were lined up on an awkward, lopsided wooden table behind him.

"What's in those jars?"

"Cha Cha."

"Cha Cha? What's that?" It looked like coleslaw in clear brine.

He scratched his chin and stared at the jars. "Oh...it's sort of a salad that folks around here make. The missus makes it from stuff we grow in our garden."

"Why is it called 'Cha Cha'?"

"Don't know. That's what my momma called it and her momma before that." He looked at me quizzically. "You don't have to know what something *is* to enjoy it."

Chapter 12

**"You find out more about a man
by listening to his conversation
than by looking at a house he
has built."**

C. S. Lewis
Mere Christianity

HOME, SWEET HOME

As I drove north through the Carolinas, Carl Sandburg's name popped into my mind. I vaguely remembered he had lived in the tiny town of Flat Rock, North Carolina, in the foothills of the Blue Ridge Mountains.

When I was a kid, after I outgrew my Brenda Starr phase, I fell in love with the American poet Carl Sandburg in a high school literature class. Everything he wrote—fiction, non-fiction, poetry or a screenplay—was brave and gritty and real. I loved the way he celebrated work and friends and love and railed unapologetically against injustice. He had something to say and people listened. Isn't that what we all secretly hope for?

I had never told anyone how I felt about him. What self-conscious teen wants to admit her hero is an old white-haired poet? The dork factor was too high. But now I realized I could visit his nearby home and indulge my curiosity about how the great poet/writer lived.

*   *   *

The Sandburg house, barns, and land were modest by almost any standard. The farm sat atop a foothill overlooking a small lake and hundreds of trees below. Sandburg named the "estate" Connemara after a district in Ireland. It's now a national historic landmark managed by the National Park Service.

Sandburg's beloved wife Paula identified Flat Rock as a possible home in 1943 using weather charts. She wanted to move the family from Michigan to a warmer climate where she could spend more time outdoors raising her prize-winning Chikaming goats and her talented husband could write undistracted. Connemara was, by all accounts, a perfect environment for both.

Sandburg's family quickly carved out a daily routine to accommodate their goals. Each night around 11 p.m. Paula and their daughters went off to bed and Sandburg retired to his cluttered office where he wrote all night.

Around 5 a.m. Paula woke up and tended to the goats and Sandburg went to bed. He slept until noon when the entire family would gather for their main meal and listen to what he had written the night before.

After lunch, he walked the foothills, answered letters, prepared for speaking engagements or read. He reportedly subscribed to more than 50 magazines and the house was crammed with 14,000 books that filled every available nook and cranny of the house. In the evenings he led impromptu family "sings," providing accompaniment on his guitar.

As I toured the grounds and listened to the docents talk about Sandburg's life story, it ignited my closeted writer's spirit with important clues about the keys to his success.

Sandburg wasn't so much courageous as he was resourceful. He didn't strike out on his own until a crisis forced him from a more traditional, financially secure career. He worked as a reporter for the *Chicago Daily News* until the Depression hit. When the newspaper cut his pay in half, he quit and became a traveling performer—reading his poetry, playing the guitar, and singing folk songs.

Once he figured out his calling and what he had to say, he set out to rearrange his life to make it happen. When he arrived at Connemara, he was ready. Plus, he had Paula. It helps to have someone hold up your picture of paradise when your own arms get tired.

He proved age doesn't matter if you have a clear vision for your life. It had been his dream since the age of 12 to write about Abraham Lincoln. Yet his six-volume Pulitzer Prize-winning Lincoln biography wasn't written until he was in his 50s. It was worth waiting for. One-third of his life's work was produced after age 67.

He wrote about what mattered to him and what he thought should matter to us. He wrote earthy tributes to the working man and scathing indictments of powerful people who abused them. He wrote vulnerable poems about his deep love for Paula and he wrote children's tales to honor the wide-eyed wonder of youth. ("The stars are so far away," he wrote, "they never speak when spoken to.")

He told the truth and didn't fear being misunderstood. Even people who didn't agree with him had to admit he seemed to understand them more than they understood themselves. His Lincoln biography deconstructed the mythic President and described a flesh and blood man whose life reflected depression and failure as well as success.

*   *   *

Heavy rains turned into a torrential downpour by the time I reached Asheville. After stops in search of lodging at nearly a dozen chain motels, I pulled into a seedy-looking place where the night clerk offered their last available room for $85. It was a waterbed.

"Why so much?" I asked.

"It's the peak fall colors weekend."

"Wait a minute. When I came through this area two weeks ago the motel clerks said the same thing. The peak colors are over! Besides, I can't afford $85. Can you recommend someplace else in the area?"

"Nobody has rooms tonight. There's a big trucker's convention going on, plus 70,000 people are attending the annual furniture shows in Hickory and High Point."

"But High Point and Hickory are over 100 miles away!"

"Lady, some people are staying on the other side of the mountain in Gatlinburg and driving back across the mountain every day. I'm telling you there are no rooms for 75 miles."

*   *   *

I circled back to the Holiday Inn to ask if I could camp in their parking lot without prompting a call to police about some car in the parking lot with a body in the back seat.

The lobby was jammed with people sitting on chairs, sofas, and every inch of available floor space—all searching for a room for the night. They passed around half a dozen phone books and took turns sharing the lobby phones.

I approached the night manager behind the front desk with my most winning smile.

"Okay, tell me that behind Door #2 there's a room with my name on it."

He looked genuinely pained. "Ma'am, trust me. I could retire on what I've been offered tonight if I could come up with a room."

"Are there any bed and breakfast places in the area that aren't booked?"

"Those were taken hours ago. We've called everywhere trying to find rooms for these people."

I noticed a crudely produced flyer rolled up in his hand that had a drawing of a house and a phone number across the top.

"Is that flyer in your hand advertising available rooms?"

"Oh, that." He looked at the roll as if he'd forgotten he was holding it. "Someone dropped it off a couple hours ago. "No one's ever heard of them. I don't like to recommend any place I haven't checked out. They might not be legitimate."

"I'm desperate. Do you mind if I check them out? What's the worst thing that can happen? I'll waste a little time. At this point, time is all I've got."

"Okay. But I can't be responsible."

"No problem. I'll pretend the motel fairy tucked it under my windshield wipers."

The woman who answered the phone said she had one small room left with a bath in the hall for $60 cash. "I've closed my corporate account for the season," she said. "I leave for Florida tomorrow."

I took it, abandoning plans to make it contingent on inspection. Unless she was an ax murderer, I'd make it work. I really didn't want to sleep in my car.

When I found the house, off a winding forested road, a buxom middle-aged woman in flip-flops and Bermuda shorts came to the door carrying a large raw Porterhouse steak in a wire basket. She was getting ready to cook it in her living room fireplace.

She showed me to my room, which, it turned out, was her bedroom. She planned to camp out on the living room sofa for the extra $60.

She started to move her clothes out of the closet to make room for mine. But when she noticed I brought in only a small overnight bag, she abandoned the idea and left her clothes where they were.

"I don't really have anywhere else to put them anyway," she said, without apology. "Oh, by the way, there's no heat. I turned it off since I'm leaving tomorrow. You can use the space heater until you go to sleep. Just remember to turn it off." I didn't ask how I was supposed to turn off the space heater if I was asleep.

She gave me a tour of the rest of the house and filled me in on the other guests—the couple with the crying baby in the room next to mine, the two ladies from Mississippi who asked for her cheapest room, even though they were driving a brand-new Cadillac, and the two guests sitting by the fire in the living room.

She said she wished they'd go to bed, for Pete's sake, so she could cook her steak.

The house with its Great Room view of the Blue Ridge Mountains must have been magnificent in its prime. But its best days had long come and gone.

I crawled into bed with my clothes on, hoping the night would quickly pass. It didn't. Long, slow-moving freight trains made regular passes by my window all night.

Our buffet breakfast in the formal dining room the next morning consisted of the remains of a box of Count Chocula cereal, grocery store doughnuts, and Tang. Whoever got there first got to eat. The coffee was served in an elegant silver carafe but tasted like tar. The whole scene was a bizarre mash-up of Martha Stewart and the Beverly Hillbillies.

During breakfast, our hostess regaled us with a non-stop monologue of her life, her former career, her adult children's lives, and her marriages—including a comprehensive recitation of the sins of each husband. There were three.

The Husband Chronicles were followed by *In-Law News*, *Government Officials Who Should Be Shot*, and *Woes of the Family Dog* (a poor critter allegedly forced to hunt for wild game when a certain live-in relative refused to feed him while our hostess was out of town). Her final monologue was a pitch to buy her house since she now lived in Florida most of the year.

She was a living example of the line, "I'm talking and I can't shut up!" She was also living proof there's no correlation between the number of words we speak and the amount of wisdom they contain.

One by one the other guests slipped out without any attempt to say goodbye and I became her only audience. At the first sign of pause, I chucked my doughnut and said I really needed to hit the road.

Minutes later I was forced back inside to ask for her help. In my haste to get in out of the rain the night before, I had left the light on inside my car. My battery was dead. She followed me outside— still talking—and pulled her fancy sports car nose-to-nose with my car.

Like everything inside the house, the hood of her car was also broken. She propped it open with a couple of expensive golf clubs and connected the jumper cables like a pro.

After my car started, she explained matter-of-factly that her car had no reverse gear. I would have to back out of the circle drive and down the long driveway. That bit of news launched a new monologue about the implications of driving a car with no reverse gear.

"It takes a little extra planning since you can't back up. Of course, parallel parking is out."

Of course.

I fled to the nearest gas station, pulled off to one side with the engine running to give my battery time to recharge, and closed my eyes in an attempt to erase the absurdity of the last 24 hours.

Anyone who believes real life is less interesting than fiction just isn't paying attention.

Chapter 13

"Certain experiences may be transmitted
by language, others—more profound—by
silence; and then there are those that
cannot be transmitted, not even by silence.
They must be lived. That's all."

Elie Wiesel
Souls on Fire

INNOCENCE IN THE BALANCE

I spent the day in Asheville waiting for 19 rolls of film to be developed. By the time the pictures were ready, it was too late to make it to Roanoke, Virginia before nightfall. I stopped instead in Elkin, North Carolina, near the Virginia border and spent a quiet evening organizing photographs and calculating trip expenses.

A quick tally to date: 3,400 miles traveled, 27 rolls of film, a jam-packed journal, and a thousand memories. I had learned so much, even if it didn't fit into some tidy Life Plan.

The next morning the growing pile of dirty clothes in the trunk sent me in search of the nearest Laundromat.

The local Washerama featured rows of well-worn washers and dryers and a grim hodge-podge of plastic bucket chairs that backed up to the front windows.

The only patrons in the place were a young mother and her little boy. A small-screen TV mounted out of reach high on the wall, blared at head-banging levels.

I separated my clothes into a couple of machines and scanned the room for soap dispensers.

131

"Say, aren't there usually machines that sell detergent in these places?" I asked.

"I don't rightly think they got any," the young woman said, looking up from her *Soap Opera Digest*. "I bring my own. You can use mine. I've got plenty. Josh, give the nice lady the Tide out of my basket over there."

The sandy-haired boy, about six or seven years old, laid down his Power Ranger coloring book and jumped up to help.

"Thanks," I said. "Let me pay you something for it. I would have had to buy some anyway."

"No need. It's just nice to have some company."

I loaded the machines with detergent and quarters and sat down next to them on one of the uncomfortable chairs.

"Are you from these parts?" she asked.

"No, I'm from Chicago."

"Whatcha doin' in Elkin?"

"Just passing through. I'm on a trip, taking pictures."

"Are you with that National Gee-o-graphic magazine? We ain't got no elephants around here!" She laughed.

"No, I'm just like taking pictures of nature."

"...ya been out to Stone Mountain?"

"Near Atlanta?" I asked.

"Have they got one there, too?" she said. "No, this one's about 20 miles due west and a little north. If you like purty scenery ya gotta see it. One whole side of it is like a flat piece of marble. My husband drove me over there on our honeymoon. That was a while ago. He's long gone, but the old mountain's still there and it's still purty."

Her son sidled up to me.

"My name's Josh. Want me to read you one of my Power Rangers books?"

At least a dozen various kinds of Power Rangers workbooks lay at his feet, along with a Power Rangers lunch box and cap.

"I don't know much about Power Rangers," I said. "'Sesame Street' and 'Mister Rogers' Neighborhood' were my daughter's favorite shows when she was your age."

"I can teach you about them!" he said, his eyes widening with excitement. He closed his Crayola box, grabbed a Power Rangers fanzine, and pulled up a chair to face me. Like a tutor grilling a student on multiplication tables, he began our lesson.

"Okay. There are six rangers. Tommy, Trini, Kimberly, Zack, Billy, and Jason. They each have their own colored outfit so you can tell them apart." He leaned toward me, cupping his hand around his mouth. His voice turned to a whisper. "But that's only when they're using their secret powers. Otherwise, they're just teenagers. But don't tell anybody about their secret identity or they'll be in danger!"

"Okay," I nodded as I crossed my heart. "I promise."

Mimicking a tone that was probably his teacher's, he turned to the beginning of his fanzine and launched again into the lesson.

"Now, Tommy's Power Ranger uniform is **white** (even though his used to be green. But that's a whole other story.) Trini's uniform is **yellow**. Kimberly's is **pink**. Zack's is **black**. Jennifer's is **red**. Billy's is **blue**. Jason's is **red**. Let's see how many you remember."

He opened one of the workbooks to a page with a Power Ranger dressed in pink and held it open up against his chest.

"Now, who is the **pink** Power Ranger?" he said in a patronizing voice. "Her name begins with a K—Kuh...Kuh...Kuh...Kimberly!" he said, sounding it out to help me. "That's right! You get a happy face!"

He reached into his book bag, retrieved a yellow Happy Face sticker and slapped it on my hand. "Very good! Now...let's try the others."

I failed miserably on every question, but my patient tutor was undeterred.

"Okay, now... let's move on to our next lesson." He laid down the first book and reached for another. "The bad guys are the Putty

People and the evil Rita Repulsa. Can you say Rita Re-pul-sa? Go ahead, let me hear you say it?"

The screaming TV volume began to get to me. "Josh, I need a quick recess so I can turn down the TV."

I stood on a chair but wasn't tall enough to reach the dials. He rushed to my aid with a bunch of old phone books, placed them on the chair to add height, and then positioned his feet as backstops so the chair wouldn't move as I adjusted the dials.

With the volume down, my pint-sized instructor resumed our lesson in earnest, until he saw his mom stand up to fold her last load of laundry. He patted my knee and said solemnly, "We have just enough time to work on our Spanish. Now repeat after me."

He recited numbers 1-50 in Spanish as he helped his mom fold the towels. I dutifully echoed each number, not wanting to risk a detention or, worse yet, the loss of another Happy Face sticker.

As his mom loaded the car, Josh stood in front of me with his hands of his hips. "You need a lot more work, but I'm willing to help you. You'll have to come to my house." He pointed out the window in the direction of an apartment building a half block away. "We live just down the street in #1-D."

With a flourish, he scooped up his book bag, waved a joyous goodbye, and skipped toward the door. "Now don't be a stranger," he said, shaking his forefinger at me. "Remember, we're in #1-D!"

I sat back down on the uncomfortable dinette chair and smiled. His teacher deserved a raise. Children like Josh remind us what we were supposed to be like before the world messed us up. I missed him before they ever left the parking lot.

A smartly dressed middle-aged man pushed through the doorway, dragging three duffel bags of laundry. He loaded several washing machines and sat down next to me, staring off into space.

"Is that your car with the Illinois plates?" he finally said.

"Yes, it is."

"You don't see too many out-of-state people in this Laundromat," he said. He didn't look like he belonged there either.

"I'm just passing through," I said. "The motel didn't have laundry facilities for guests."

"Our family is relatively new in the area, too. We haven't hooked up the washer and dryer yet."

"Where are you from?" I asked.

"Atlanta. I used to be a high school teacher."

"Do you teach here now?"

"No, I got out of the profession. Toward the end, I wasn't doing much teaching anyway. All my time was spent trying to control the classroom. I didn't get a masters degree in education to be a policeman." His tone carried a deep sadness.

"What brought you to Elkin?"

"My wife's a nurse anesthetist. Small town hospitals pay big bucks for her skills. She got a great job offer, so we packed up our three kids and moved."

"Do you like it here?"

He put his elbows on his legs and leaned over, staring at the floor. "Oh, the people are nice. And it's safe. But there's a lot I miss—like stimulating conversation, professional theatre, ethnic restaurants. This isn't exactly the epicenter of culture."

He let out a long sigh. "I guess you never know how something will turn out until you try it."

"I'm sorry it hasn't worked out for you."

"You gain a lot by moving to a small town," he said, "but you lose a lot, too. I don't think we calculated for that part. On paper, it seemed like a good decision. But now? Well...not so much."

"So what do you do for a living in Elkin?"

"I'm a broker," he said, without enthusiasm.

I didn't ask what kind of broker. It was clear he didn't like the work and would do anything else at the first opportunity.

He asked what books I was reading and whether I had ever read anything by C.S. Lewis. A friend had given him a copy of the famed author's *Screwtape Letters*. He loved Lewis's satirical use of reverse psychology to show how people obsess over their own importance while envying the success of others.

"My wife thinks satire is a dumb way to communicate spiritual truth," he concluded, "but it sure nailed me."

An awkward silence fell between us as the washing machines hummed in the background. I wasn't quite sure how to respond. I love C. S. Lewis and could have engaged in a discussion of his books, but I didn't think that's what he needed.

"I want to do something extraordinary, you know?" he finally said. "Maybe not extraordinary as in 'successful,' but something that matters—something that makes a difference." He looked at me with a pained expression. "I guess that's what we all want, isn't it?"

I explained my trip was part of a similar quest. Then I shared a little of what I'd learned so far about myself and about life and God. But, taking a cue from the hiker at Amicalola Falls, I withheld my normal avalanche of words and let him draw his own application. I felt sorry for him. He took a risk, like the Appalachian hiker, but, in his case, it didn't turn out as he planned. I told him life rarely happens in a straight line and I hoped he wouldn't give up.

Once back on the road, two very different conversations replayed in my head: Josh, the teacher-wannabe so full of passion, hope and idealism and the burned-out teacher who has learned the road to fulfillment is uneven, sometimes unfair, and seldom a smooth ride.

*　　*　　*

The Visitor's Center at Stone Mountain resembled a giant tree house, rising at least 20 or 30 feet off the ground. It was accessible only by a steep flight of outdoor wooden stairs. A staffer explained that the height allowed visitors to see the distant sheer granite face of the mountain without taking the strenuous two-mile hike to the overlook.

I took a few snapshots of the mountain from atop the Center but didn't stay long. I didn't have the right long-distance photo lens to get any decent shots.

As I hastily sprinted back down the steps to my car, I failed to see the peach-sized tree knot that had fallen onto one of the stairs. My right foot stepped on it and spun out from under me, sharply twisting my ankle. I should have fallen backward, but instead—for some inexplicable reason—I fell forward. Instinctively, my hands flew out in front of me as I slammed to the ground several steps below with a nasty thud. Every part of my body felt assaulted.

I began to yell for help, certain my ankle was broken. Because of the park's small size and the mountain's limited accessibility, it's not a major tourist stop, especially in the off-season. The only person in the vicinity was the lone employee in the Visitor's Center at the top of the long flight of steps and at the opposite end of the building. She didn't hear a thing.

The pain took my breath away. Whimpering, I curled onto my side, trying to stay calm and alert. My camera lay off to one side, dented, but in one piece because it landed on a mound of dirt.

Several minutes later a pickup truck pulled into the parking lot. When the driver saw me sprawled on the ground moaning, he flung open the door of his truck and ran toward me.

"Are you alright? What happened? Don't move. I'll call for help." He was the Center's maintenance man. He grabbed his two-way radio to call for an ambulance.

"No, no....please," I said. "It will take at least 20-30 minutes for an ambulance to get here and the same amount of time to return to the hospital, right? I can't bear to wait that long. Can't you just take me to the hospital in your truck? I'm in horrible pain."

"I don't know if we should move you," he said.

"I didn't fall on my back or my neck. I'm conscious. I'm not seeing double. I think I'm just badly banged up, except for my foot."

He radioed the woman inside the Visitor's Center. Together they carried me inside a nearby storage area where he gently took off my shoe and sock and made a makeshift splint from a first-aid kit. The woman asked me to write down what happened before we left so she could file a report.

Oh, sure. I'll get right on that...right after I scream for about 20 more minutes from the pain.

They both sheepishly explained that the state carried no liability insurance for anyone injured in a state park, so I would be paying my own medical bills.

"Honey, I'm so sorry," she said. "We've got to do something about those stairs. You're the second person who's fallen today." Together they carried me to the truck and we sped off to the Hugh Chatham Medical Center.

ER nurses wrapped me in heated blankets and took vital signs. A physician methodically inventoried my injuries.

"Young lady, you're supposed to do all your falling off the mountain, not the visitor's station."

"Doc," I said, gritting my teeth, "I'm in a boatload of hurt. Can you give me a shot of something? I promise never to tell another dumb doctor joke again!"

He ordered an opiate and x-rays and said, "I suspect you've got a bad sprain or a hairline fracture. I know it sounds strange, but a sprain can be more painful than a break. I have to warn you the second-day pain is usually worse than the first."

He turned to the nurse. "Give her a Jones wrap and fit her with crutches. If the x-rays show a full break, we'll worry later about a cast."

The park maintenance man and his boss transported me back to the motel where I had stayed the previous night and checked out. Then they went back and retrieved my car and belongings from the Visitor's Center and unloaded everything that I might need for the next several days onto the second bed in my motel room.

The meds made me spacey but I was grateful to be out of pain, in a safe place, and cared for by the kindness of strangers. I called George and Lisa to let them know about the accident, ordered a pizza to be delivered, and fell into a drug-induced sleep.

*　　*　　*

The doctor was right. The second day was awful. I wanted off the pills because I felt like such a zombie, but the pain won out. I staggered back and forth to the bathroom in a stupor, barely aware of the bustle around me when the maid came to clean my room.

She was glad for my company, she said, because the motel was pretty empty this time of year. The only people around—except for staff—were tradesmen working on two nearby construction projects. They stayed at the motel during the week and went home on weekends—a pattern they would continue for at least two to three more months.

I couldn't focus enough to read. After several hours of mindless TV, I grabbed my crutches and decided to test my maneuverability by hobbling to the ice machine at the end of the breezeway, hoping the fresh air would clear my mental fog.

I didn't think through how I was going to hold onto the crutches and carry a bucket of ice on the return trip. Laboriously, I inched my way back to the room. When I reached my door I propped the ice bucket against the wall with my stomach, draped both arms over the cumbersome crutches and fished for my room key. A cherubic-looking man rushed to my aid.

"Hey, a pretty little lady like you should have someone else get her ice! Here, let me hold that."

As I fumbled for the door lock, he took the ice bucket, told me his name, and explained that he was staying at the motel for 13 weeks while working nearby on a construction assignment. Apparently, he was one of the tradesmen the maid had mentioned.

Once opened, the heavy metal door kept wanting to close. I leaned against it to keep it ajar and turned to take the ice from him.

"Thanks for your help. I can take it from here. I haven't quite gotten the hang of these crutches. I feel like a centipede."

He leaned into the door to hold it open. "Go on in, darlin.' I'll hold the door."

I stepped across the threshold into the room, then turned to take the ice bucket. He walked past me to set the bucket on the dresser, letting the door slam behind him.

"You looked like you needed some extra hands and I'm glad to help. Here, let me help you get settled." His tone was empathetic. He kept up a steady stream of idle chatter as he walked over to the bed and pulled out the pillows to prop them against the headboard.

Exhausted by the walk to the ice machine and still disoriented from the medication, I hobbled to the edge of the bed, laid down the crutches, swung my bandaged leg up on the bed, and sunk back into the pillows.

He casually walked over and sat down on a chair, positioning himself between the door and me. In a heart-stopping nanosecond my brain sprang into full alert.

I'm in a motel room with a total stranger in a town no one's ever heard of. I'm spaced out on medication and unable to run. He's bigger than me, no one knows he's here, and he has the door blocked.

"They've got a bunch of us staying here workin' on the new shirt factory down the road," he said warmly. "Between us and the other guys who stay here who are working on that utility project, we don't see many pretty ladies. You're going to be laid up for a few days. Why don't you let me buy you dinner? Then we can come back here and talk."

I struggled to sound nonchalant. "Thanks, but I don't feel like eating. Besides, I'm really tired. And when this pain medicine wears off I'm not going to be fit company. I'd appreciate it if you'd leave now so I can take a nap. Thanks for the invitation."

He made no move to get up.

"I'll tell you what. Why don't you just go right ahead and nap, and I'll sit right here and look at your pretty little face. Then when you wake up we can go have a bite to eat. I insist."

My heart began to race. The phone was across the room where he had moved it, so I wouldn't trip over the cord with my crutches.

"Look," I said, as firmly as I could muster, "You've been very kind. I'm sure you're a straight-ahead kind of guy. But that's not going to happen. I'm not comfortable having you in my room and I don't go to dinner with strangers. I'm happily married and I..."

"Well, see? That's another thing we have in common," he interrupted. "At least I used to be married. Here...I've got a picture of her."

He whipped out a well-worn wallet from the hip pocket of his jeans and pulled out a color photograph that looked like it was taken in the 1950s. Then he pulled out pictures of his adult children and launched into a description of each of them and what they did for a living, followed by a rundown on his young grandchildren. He didn't look old enough to have grandchildren.

"Have you got a picture of your husband?" he asked.

My mind raced in search of an "out," but he beat me to the punch. His eye caught the picture of George and me displayed on the nightstand. He came over and sat down on the edge of the bed next to me to get a closer look.

My heart started pounding so hard I could barely breathe. I held on tightly to the bedspread to keep my hands from trembling.

"Is that you and him?" he said warmly.

"I'm sorry," I said, "but I think I'm going to throw up. It must be all those meds. Will you please hand me my crutches?"

"Let me give you my arm, darlin'."

"No!" I said, before forcing myself to sound calm. "No, I need to learn how to maneuver them on my own. Please...just hand me the crutches. I don't mean to sound so uptight, but I really don't feel well."

Reluctantly, he reached for the crutches as I swung my legs over the other side of the bed and struggled to stand upright. As quickly as possible, I stumbled into the bathroom and quietly shut and locked the door.

"I'm going to be in here a while," I shouted through the door. "I really feel sick to my stomach. Please pull the door closed on your way out, okay? Thanks again for your help."

He walked over to the bathroom door.

"Are you sure I can't help?"

"Please...leave," I said firmly through the door.

"Honey, I'm not going to do nothin' to you. We're just two lonely people and all I'm doin' is invitin' you to dinner!"

"I understand. And that's a very kind gesture. But I'm not lonely and it's not going to happen. Look, I live in a big city where having dinner with a total stranger is about as smart as putting a loaded gun to your head. I don't do it. It's nothing personal. Please...leave...now...or I'll have to start yelling and pounding on the ceiling with my crutches."

"No need to do that, sweet thing." His voice sounded hurt. "I'm leaving. I'll call you tomorrow to see how you're doin'." He wrote down his room number in case I changed my mind and then I heard the door slam shut.

Several minutes later, I hobbled out of the bathroom and fell onto the bed with relief.

Maybe he was just trying to help. I hate that we live in a world where you can't tell the Good Guys from the Bad Guys anymore.

As promised, he called every day to check in on me and see if I needed anything. I never answered his calls or responded to his messages. I never saw him again.

Chapter 14

"Don't ask yourself what the world needs. Ask yourself what makes you come alive and go do that, because what the world needs is people who have come alive."

John Eldredge
Wild at Heart

DEFINING WHAT MATTERS

The landscape changed when I crossed into Virginia. Split-rail fencing bordered the high-altitude Blue Ridge Parkway and, instead of dense forests down below, the Piedmont Valley was a checkerboard of farm fields.

At Mabry Mill, I stopped to take pictures of the old paddle-wheeled gristmill in the late afternoon sun. The flashy colors of autumn were now giving way to more somber shades of brown. Winter was definitely in the wings.

My throbbing ankle and foot demanded periodic breaks from driving. I stopped at a general store nearby and flopped down on one of the rockers on the front porch, propping my leg up on a 50-lb. sack of cabbages.

Off in the distance, a man on a tractor was hauling more cabbages to a nearby farm stand. They looked like giant green basketballs. Intrigued, several minutes later I hobbled over to get a closer look.

Two women in simple farm dresses watched me as I inched my way to the scales.

"Girl, what are you doin' trampin' around in this field with your leg all banged up!" one scolded with a smile.

I stopped to lean on my crutches, out of breath. "What if I told you it's been my lifelong dream to visit a cabbage farm?"

"Then we'd tell you to get a life!" the other one laughed. "You picked a good farm, though. I'll give you that. Amos has been farming cabbages for 11 years and his are the best you'll find. He used to farm 40 acres, but only farms a few acres now. He raises cattle on the rest. You can't make a living raising cabbages."

"Why not? Can't make enough money?"

"Yup." She pointed to the flatbed of cabbages coming toward us. "I'll bet two of those will cost you about a buck," she said.

"A dollar? You're kidding! But I don't want to buy any. I'm traveling and have no way to refrigerate them. I was just curious to know why someone would choose to farm cabbages."

"Don't expect much of an answer out of Amos. He's not the talking type. It's a shame you can't cook up a mess of his cabbage, though. It's sweeter than the stuff you get in the grocery store. His don't give you the stomach 'talk-back,' if you know what I mean. That comes from cabbages sitting for weeks in refrigerated trucks and grocery coolers. When you buy them fresh and cook them up in chicken broth, they're the best things you ever tasted! My kids would eat cabbage three meals a day if I'd let them.

"Thanks for the tip. How long do you think one of them would last in my car without spoiling? I know the weather's turning colder, but I may not be home for a while."

"Oh, they'll keep a couple weeks if you leave them in the car at night where it's cool."

"You've talked me into it."

A friendly man with a weathered face hopped off his cabbage-laden flatbed. As forewarned, he didn't want to talk and he charged a dollar for two cabbages—a small price to pay for the look I expected on George's face when I walked in the house hoisting two cabbages the size of globes.

He and George had at least one thing in common. Neither of them felt they owed strangers an explanation for their lives, even if others thought they did.

*   *   *

By the time I reached Roanoke, I was tired, hungry, and my whole body throbbed with pain from my injuries. I should have stopped at the first sign of a motel, but I drove across town instead, thinking it would save a tedious crawl through rush hour traffic the next morning. Unfortunately—in keeping with my unbroken string of motel fiascos—all the motels were on the side of town I had left behind.

I pulled into the parking lot of my only immediate hope for lodging. The place was empty, except for a group of teenagers with nose rings and nail-spiked leather wristbands. The boys were drag racing their beaters through the parking lot, as their girlfriends unloaded kegs into rooms a few doors down from mine. I declined their party invitation—uncertain what role I could possibly play besides surrogate parole officer.

I awkwardly pushed open the door to my motel room with my crutch, threw down my bag, and fell onto the bed. The doorknob was busted and wouldn't shut without hurling my body against it. The heater blew visible dirt onto the counter. I hurt so badly I couldn't even muster outrage.

*   *   *

Promoters of the Natural Bridge of Virginia call it one of the seven natural wonders of the world, but it was no prettier than the limestone bridge over Little Creek in Cadiz, Kentucky.

True, it was 215 feet tall and allegedly those were supposed to be George Washington's initials carved in the rock under the arch. But it wasn't the Parthenon. Much ado about nothing.

Local lore insisted that soldiers in the American Revolutionary army used the bridge's height to make munitions. Reportedly, they poured drops of molten lead off the top of the bridge and by the time the lead hit the water, gravity shaped the lead into bullets— bullets used to defeat the British. It's a story that ranks right up there with, "My dog ate my homework" and "The check is in the mail."

Points for creative storytelling. Another example of our deep-seated human desire to feel part of something bigger than ourselves.

I remembered several years earlier when I learned I was a direct descendant of American Revolutionary soldier Jonathan Miner, Jr., a gunner in Capt. Nathaniel Saltonstall's Company. There it was in the public record for all to see—my relative, a bona fide patriot. I probably wouldn't have cared that much about Jonathan Miner, Jr. if America hadn't won the war. But we did win, so I cared. My turn to feel part of history.

*   *   *

History is in your face everywhere in Virginia. I didn't enjoy American History in high school. So I felt I should fill in a few gaps in my education. I stopped at the restored 1860s village at Appomattox, where Gen. Robert E. Lee surrendered to Gen. Ulysses S. Grant at the end of the Civil War.

A docent dressed in the clothes of the 1860s posed as Mary Hix, daughter of the owner of the Clover Hill Tavern. The tavern had been a popular stagecoach stop between Lynchburg and Richmond during the war.

"Miss Hix" walked through the crowd describing that momentous day when Confederate soldiers assembled to acknowledge defeat. The cavalry units surrendered first, she said. Then the artillery units and the infantry followed. Both sides had suffered heavy losses. In some units as few as 60 soldiers remained, out of a company of 1,000.

Poignantly, she described how Yankee General Chamberlain ordered his soldiers to line the streets and "carry arms." When the Yankees cocked their guns, Confederate soldiers feared they were about to be shot down in cold blood. Instead, the victors were saluting them—their sworn enemy—for their valiant fight. It was a riveting acknowledgment that everyone pays a price in war, regardless of which side you're on.

The woman portraying Miss Hix finished her monologue and wandered through the crowd to answer questions. A young boy tugged at her voluminous skirt.

"Were you scared *you'd* be shot, *too?*" he said. His eyes were as big as dinner plates.

"Of course! We were all scared. Wouldn't you be?"

An older pal punched the young boy in the shoulder. "C'mon, dweeb, she's not real! She's fake. Let's go."

The younger boy stared at the woman with a puzzled look, then peered at the back of her skirt.

"What are you looking for?" the older boy asked.

"If she's not real, where did they install the batteries?"

Chapter 15

**"In a world full of fugitives,
the person taking the opposite
direction will appear to be
running away."**

T. S. Eliot

DIFFERENT STROKES

Teenagers rollerbladed around me on the boardwalk. The beach was largely deserted. Forty blocks of empty motel parking lots confirmed the tourist season in Virginia Beach was definitely over. It was, after all, almost November, a month when coastal weather is not known for being hospitable.

The momentum that had fueled my trip was gone. I felt a growing sense my days of self-reflection were coming to an end. George said I'd know when it was time to come home. Maybe it was time.

An ominous sky indicated imminent rain. I hurried down to the beach for a quick stroll, to take advantage of the unseasonably balmy temperatures and intoxicating salt sea air.

Great Danes as tall as ponies bounded toward me, chased by a group of children and a young couple trying to herd them.

"Murphy! Hogan! Get your butts back here." The petite mom turned to me with a shrug. "So much for obedience training." The two giant dogs dwarfed her.

"Those are the biggest dogs I've ever seen!" I said. "How much do they weigh?"

"About 225 lbs. each."

"Whoa! Your very own linebackers!"

"Yeah, they go through 150 lbs. of dry dog food every six weeks. That's more than my kids eat."

"Are those your kids?"

"That boy and girl are ours," she said, pointing to them. "The other two girls are their friends. The one with the frizzy hair has leukemia. She's not expected to live more than another couple of months. Sweet kid. She loves the beach, so we try to bring her out here as often as possible."

She explained she worked with terminally ill kids at a hospital in Washington, DC, but was on temporary medical leave because of a shoulder injury.

"We're beach people. My husband gets out of the service next year and we're hoping to move to Florida."

Her sullen husband stood a few steps behind her, ignoring our conversation, content to hide behind his Ray-Bans.

"Say," I said to him, "Last night I got lost driving around the north end of Virginia Beach. I ended up on some backroad on military property. MPs stopped me and escorted me off the property so quickly I felt lucky not to be arrested! Is that some kind of off-limits area?"

He stared straight ahead and assumed an "at ease" stance.

"Wouldn't know, ma'am." He might as well have been wearing a "Do Not Enter" sign on his chest. I'm sure he had a story to tell, but he wasn't telling it to me.

The Danes set off running again—their human entourage in hot pursuit—sparing Stoic Man from further interrogation.

As I watched them disappear in the distance, two elderly men nearly bowled me over from behind. They wore headphones and carried long rods with disks on the end that were tethered to battery packs. Walking with heads down, they were oblivious to anyone in their path.

"You fellas must be on a mission!" I said. "Those are pretty hip walking sticks you're using. Are those radios rigged to the canes?"

"Nope. They're metal detectors—$700 apiece," one of them said. "We walk the beach looking for stuff people have lost. Been doing it for 23 years."

"What kind of stuff do you find?" I asked.

"Oh, rings, watches, stuff like that. We found a fancy diver's watch once." He pulled an odd-shaped coin out of his pocket and flipped up his sunshades to better scrutinize his latest find. "This morning we found some foreign coins."

"So what do you do with the stuff? Clean it up and sell it?"

"Nope," he said. "We swap it at our collectors' club, the Tidewater Coin and Relic Club. If we made money off it, then the FBI and the CIO (sic) might come after us!

"Nice to make your acquaintance," the other one said with a grin. They tipped their caps and resumed their heads-down stroll.

*　　*　　*

Lunch at Ocean Eddie's gave me a bird's-eye view of the crabbers stationed along the pier and the surfers in wetsuits who were pacing the beach studying the swells. Over and over again the surfers dropped their boards into the water and paddled out to catch an express ride back to shore.

A teenager in a faded T-shirt and cutoffs sat down at the table next to me. He wore a silver earring and carried smokes in his hip pocket. He seemed a million miles away, never taking his eyes off the surfers as he nursed a Coke and fries. We were the only patrons in the restaurant.

"Do you surf?" I finally asked.

"Yeah, but not these wimpy waves. You've got to be out here at dawn or late in the day when the tide rolls in to catch the good waves."

"Which is better—morning or evening?"

"About 5:30 in the morning. The winds are outgoing blowing in from west/southwest. A storm is even better. Then you can catch some eight-foot waves and 20-foot swells. It's not The Pipeline, but it's pretty good for around here."

"What's The Pipeline?"

"It's a famous surfing area in Hawaii. The waves are awesome."

We watched the surfers for several minutes in silence.

"I've always wondered how surfers 'catch a wave'," I finally said.

"You duck-dive into the oncoming wave and come out the back side of it," he explained. "Then you do a roundhouse cutback and turn into the wave and ride its face. If you're good, you come up on the lip of the wave and the wave sends you airborne for a few seconds. But, if you don't hit it just right, the waves can kill you."

His face turned somber. "I've had a few scares." He lifted his right arm to bare a jagged scar about six inches long.

"I caught someone else's board." He shrugged. "...some doofus who never should have been out there in the first place did a 'flying Wallenda' about two seconds after he stood up. So did his board."

"How long have you been surfing?"

"Since I was 10. I don't know what I'll do when I get too old to do it anymore. Surfers are like junkies. We can't get enough of the water. I wake up every morning before the sun comes up to watch The Weather Channel, to see if it might be a good day to ride. Hurricane season is the best. The waves are twice their normal size. It's an adrenaline rush that's better than sex, bungee jumping, and a roller coaster combined."

"Makes me sorry I never tried it!" I grinned. "Wait, who am I kidding? I could drown treading water! I'm pretty sports-challenged. Definitely not a person to chase danger. Real life is scary enough."

"Real life is scarier," he said, staring off into the horizon. "I understand the waves. I don't do stupid things when I'm out there. But I don't understand life."

"Well, that makes two of us." More silence. I thought about what I would say to him if he were my son—the son I never had.

"Would you indulge me a Mom-alie?" I asked.

"A what?"

"You know, those sayings that moms tell their kids over and over, like 'Don't cross your eyes because they might stay that way.'"

"Oh yeah. Those! My mom has lots of those. Her favorite is, 'When are you going to do something with your time besides being a beach bum.'"

Tears welled up in my eyes.

"I'm sorry," he said, awkwardly. "Is that something you say to your kids?"

"No, no. It's just that I once had something that I loved doing as much as you love surfing. I stopped doing it because—like your mom—my dad thought it, too, was pointless. I've spent the last 30-40 years trying to find something to do that would get everyone off my back so I could get back to what I love. It wasn't like I wanted to rob banks or something. I just didn't see the world the way other people saw it."

He nodded in agreement and let out a deep sigh, turning his attention back to the ocean.

"Hey," I finally said, "I don't even know your name, but ..."

"It's Jeff."

"Jeff, look...." I paused, searching for words. "I don't want to undermine your mom's words. I'm a mom, too. I know what it's like to be in her shoes. But what you said about loving the water? That's important information. It's a clue. I don't know exactly what it means in the context of your future, but somewhere in your life you have to find a way to honor what it's telling you about who you are. It's a clue. You have to exercise that 'bent.' Otherwise, a part of you will die."

"I always wanted to be a writer or a photographer or something really creative. It kept bubbling up in everything I did, but I ignored it. It was easier to ignore than Dad's pressure.

"I'm sure he felt he was doing me a favor, saving me from making a terrible mistake. He was a product of the Depression. To him, financial success was the best way to win in life. Run harder than the next guy. Make a lot of money so circumstances never gain the upper hand. In his mind, people in the creative arts didn't stand a chance. But do you want to hear something bizarre?"

"What?" he said.

"When he died we were going through his papers and came upon a box of mementos from his college days. He used to write poetry! It blew me away. He was not a man you could ever imagine writing poetry. None of us knew! I'm not suggesting he should have been (or could have been) a poet instead of a businessman. But he let that part of himself die, even though those poems apparently mattered enough to him to save them for half a century.

"He was not a happy man. I wonder if he would have been a different person if he had fed those parts of himself that he starved instead."

Jeff looked at me with sad eyes. "It feels like a no-win situation."

"How so?" I asked.

"...like you either do what really makes you happy and have all the 'I'm-older-than-you-and-I-know-what's-best-for-you' people in your life write you off, or you do what everybody expects and you're p---ed off about it the rest of your life."

He put his elbows on the table and rested his chin in his hands. "My parents would have a cow if they heard me say this," he said, "but I know they love me. I know they want me happy. We just don't have the same definition of happy."

"Jeff, all I know is that I haven't been doing what I love most or do best and I've paid a high price for it. When you ignore your passions and the things that make your heart beat fast, something inside of you goes on a restless search for that part of you that's missing-in-action. Nothing satisfies until you find it and do something about it.

"On the other hand, I have a husband, a daughter, friends—the whole nine yards—and I don't plan to throw all that overboard and run off and join a commune in order to do it."

"So what are you going to do?" he said.

"I'm not sure yet. I'm still figuring that out. All I know at the moment is that I'm going to take my best shot at finding a way to do both. I know it will cost me...and I accept that it may take awhile. That's okay. It will give everybody—including me—time to test the new direction and get used to the change. Somebody is bound to get their shorts in a knot because I'm disturbing their definition of what women my age are supposed to do. I thought the world would be so *over* that by now, but I've learned people 'tsk-tsk' just as loudly when you're 50 as they do when you're 17. They say things like, 'What a shame. She had such promise. Why would she want to go and do that?' Sound familiar?"

"Yeah. I was in the top 10% of my class," Jeff answered, "and everybody had my life mapped out before I even graduated. But nobody asked me what *I* wanted o do."

He stared forlornly out at the ocean. "Heck, what do I know? Maybe they're right."

He turned and looked at me. "So how far are you willing to go to do what you love?"

"I don't know," I answered. "Does anyone know at the front end of a decision exactly how he'll handle what comes next? Besides, life can blindside you when you're doing exactly what everyone expects of you, too."

He nodded sympathetically.

"I've been thinking about this a lot lately," I said, "about how life doesn't unfold in a straight line. If I can't make it work? Well, at least I will have tried. I'd rather be accused of pushing back against all the "oughts" in my life than to be known for rolling over and playing dead."

He glanced at his watch, jumped up, and said he had to leave for work at a place further down the beach. "Good luck on your trip." He wadded his trash. "Who knows where we'll both be in five years."

"Maybe I'll see you on ESPN riding The Pipeline," I said, "...or on the Discovery Channel leading marine biologists on some exciting underwater exploration."

He grinned, held up his hand for a high five, and left.

*   *   *

Rolling out of bed in my motel room the next morning, I stepped into water half an inch deep. The floater in the toilet tank broke in the middle of the night and gallons of water had poured over the side of the toilet onto the bathroom and bedroom floor. I didn't hear it happen because of earplugs I used to filter out noise from adjacent rooms.

Another motel from hell. I sat on the edge of the bed for another ugly cry.

*   *   *

I stopped for lunch at a café near the entrance to the Chesapeake Bay Bridge. It was Halloween and all the waitresses were in costume. A table of soldiers mercilessly razzed one attractive blonde waitress over her costume of Army fatigues.

"Hey, doll, don't you know you're not supposed to wear fatigues unless you're in the military." The recruit with the buzz haircut looked like he'd been in the service about two hours.

"So arrest me," she countered, sweeping past him to take my order.

"Is that how they show you the love?" I said.

"I used to be a WAC and they know it. I just ignore them. It drives them crazy. I call the tall guy 'Private Butt-in-ski.' If his mouth stayed open very long, his brains would fall out."

I ate quickly, hoping to cross the 17-mile-long bridge to the Delmarva Peninsula before the increasing clouds spoiled any chance for pictures.

Since I missed seeing the wild ponies on Ocracoke earlier on the trip because of the tropical storm, I hoped to see the wild ponies that reportedly roamed the Chincoteague National Wildlife Refuge on the barrier island east of the peninsula.

According to legend, tiny horses fell off a 17th Century Spanish galleon that capsized in a hurricane off the New England coast. They swam for their lives to the islands and were later romanticized in Marguerite Henry's classic children's book, *Misty of Chincoteague*.

Cynics say the island ponies are nothing more than abandoned farm animals that destroy the marsh grasses and sea oats that hold the dunes in place and provide a nesting place for endangered birds. Nevertheless, the legend endures. The U.S. Fish and Wildlife Service protects them in a 13,000-acre natural wilderness corral.

Halfway across the bridge, a heavy fog rolled in, wiping out any trace of the horizon. I felt disoriented with no sense of top and bottom or left and right. The bridge's guardrail—the only thing that separated me from 75-foot-deep waters below—was barely visible.

The unrelenting weather and motel issues were really wearing me down. My longing for home, friends, family, and continuity began to trump the allure of whatever adventure awaited me around the next corner.

Heron, snowy egrets, and other exotic birds stood stoically in the salt marshes as the darkening clouds cast their spell over the barren out-island. The ponies were nowhere in sight, apparently hiding out on the part of the island that was inaccessible to cars.

I parked behind one of the dunes that served as a barrier to the ocean and climbed up on the crest to watch the waves as they intensified.

The tall marsh grasses, like a good dance partner, swayed in perfect rhythm with the accelerating wind. Their languid sway gave no hint of the ferocity of the coming storm.

They made it look so easy, going with the flow. I envied their resilience.

By the time I calculate every risk, life has found another partner. I guess that's the price you pay for playing it safe. You wake up and realize you didn't get to dance.

I sprinted for the car as winds began to whip the ocean into a frenzy. Young men in wetsuits dashed past me up the backside of the dune with their surfboards.

"It's pretty rough out there!" I shouted to them over the sound of the crashing waves.

"Yeah, isn't it great!" one answered. I shook my head and barely made it to the car before the downpour began.

*   *   *

The National Weather Service warned of severe weather for the next 48-72 hours. I wanted off the islands. I hurried to the bridge that connects the Delmarva Peninsula to Annapolis, Maryland, hoping to get out ahead of the storm.

I turned on WTOP-AM, the all-news radio station in Washington, DC, to get a weather update. Their meteorologist warned of 60-70 mile-an-hour winds on the peninsula. They also reported a tornado-like cloud had passed through Baltimore 15 minutes earlier, taking the roofs off 100 homes and heavily damaging an eight-block area. It was heading southeast toward the bridge. Newscasters urged motorists to stay off the bridge until the storm passed.

I was already on the bridge with no way to turn back. Off to the right, I saw a wide black cloud in the distance, rolling in behind the driving rains and high winds. My heart began to race.

That's when I noticed them—two semis had slipped into position as my forward and rear guard, reprising their role from that dark night in Appalachia. They chaperoned me to safety, and, after we made it across the bridge, they blended into mainland traffic and disappeared.

Chapter 16

"No trumpets sound when the
important decisions of our life
are made. Destiny is made known
silently."

Agnes DeMille

FINISHED BUSINESS

It was as if someone said, "Strike the set!" and I was watching the takedown. One by one, state park lodges and ranger stations were closing for the season. Road crews along the northern end of the Blue Ridge Parkway worked frantically to make final repairs before winter's formal arrival. The days were getting shorter. The sun had not made an appearance for a week.

I lost all interest in taking pictures or engaging people in conversation. All my questions weren't answered, but I had enough to chew on for quite a while. I had been working on listening more consciously to what my life was trying to tell me. Standing on the edge of Dickey Ridge, instinctively I knew. It was time to go home.

I leaned back against the car to buffer myself against the harsh wind as I studied the fast-moving clouds. The sky was beautiful, an oozing kaleidoscope of shapes and colors. It was like nature's warning that a seasonal change was coming—a good metaphor for my transition back to reality.

I've always hated change, but I see it differently now. Change is not some personal vendetta the world delivers to trip us up. It's the

161

way the world works. It's the way everything in the universe grows and renews and refreshes. I can applaud or curse it, but I can't stop it. It's God's universe, not mine.

* * *

I wandered around Front Royal, Virginia, waiting for more film to be developed. Confederate flags draped most buildings, including a storefront that billed itself as "the only tattoo parlor in Rebel Country."

Business was slow at the local coffee shop. The waitress sat down in my booth and shared a few of her favorite Civil War stories. I was killing time and actually enjoying it.

Before leaving town I called a former colleague from the corporate world to see if I could drop by for a quick visit on my way through Pennsylvania, heading toward home. They were excited for the company.

She and her husband had been in fast-track careers in Chicago before moving to a bleak steel mill town to care for a terminally ill relative. They lived high on a bluff overlooking the town in its only upscale neighborhood. Her husband was teaching business courses at a satellite campus of the University of Pittsburgh. She was pregnant with their first child.

After a warm reunion with both of them, Ann and I went out to dinner to catch up in more detail. It was my first opportunity to talk about my trip to anyone in any detail. When I phoned home each night, I typically shared only highlights with George and Lisa, saving the details for my return.

She listened attentively to all I shared and then turned serious. "Verla, I hope you realize this trip will change you forever. It may not soak in for months or even years. But everything will be different now, whether you like it or not."

She described a trip she had taken to Thailand early in her consulting career and the way it still impacted her life.

"You'll be driving someday on the expressway in horrible traffic," she said, "and the traffic won't matter. You'll think back to that experience in the storm on Bay Bridge or that incident with the flying steel rod in southern Georgia and the traffic will seem totally irrelevant. You'll feel differently about your whole life and the changes will last. They really will."

Back at the house, we browsed through my trip pictures and she and her husband suggested a couple additional interesting stops I could add to my route as I wound my way toward a westbound Interstate. I didn't make any of the stops. I wanted to keep moving toward home.

*   *   *

I did make an unplanned stop in downtown Pittsburgh when I saw Market Square, a stunning all-glass complex of buildings that was home to an international glass company. It was the sparkling centerpiece of the city with its prism-like windows that resembled finely cut gemstones. It cried out to be photographed.

I watched a Jamaican immigrant who stood alone on the plaza playing Caribbean steel pan drums with big soft mallets. The rhythms bounced off the glass with thrilling acoustical effect. He played with his eyes closed, his face reflecting utter joy.

A beefy security guard emerged from one of the buildings. He waved his two-way radio at the musician as he shouted over the music.

"Hey, pal. This is private property. You can't play here!"

The young man politely explained that he was not asking anyone for money. He simply wanted to share the beautiful music with anyone who cared to listen. This particular spot, he said, was the best spot in all Pittsburgh to play his instrument because of the way the music reverberated off the glass buildings.

"That's nice...but move along. You can't play here. It's company policy."

"Sir," I interrupted, "Why not let him play a few minutes? He's not bothering anybody and he's providing a free concert. It's beautiful!"

The guard walked over and got in my face. "Hey, lady, stay out of this! This is none of your business."

"But you're treating him like a vagrant! He's well dressed. He's not begging. It's not like he's spraying graffiti on your windows. All he's doing is filling the air with beautiful sounds!"

"You!" He pointed his two-way radio at me. "Outta here! Now!"

Reluctantly, I thanked the musician for the concert and walked back to my car as it began to rain.

Not everyone likes the gifts we bring to the world, my friend, but don't stop playing. Your audience is out there somewhere and they need you. Go find them.

Heavy storms were forecast for the rest of the day. I hit the road heading west.

*   *   *

Once settled in at the waterfront motel in Port Clinton, Ohio, I called home with my surprise announcement.

"Send away the dancing girls. I'm coming home!"

"Uh, oh," George shouted to Lisa, 'Call the exterminator. Your mom's coming home!' That's great, honey! When will you be here?"

"Day after tomorrow. I could make it by tomorrow if I drove straight through. But last night Ann and John said any trip this important deserved a special finale. They recommended their favorite bed and breakfast inn on the eastern side of Lake Michigan, so I'm going to stop there and take one last day to cement my thoughts."

"Good idea!" George said. "You realize the significance of that day, don't you?"

I mentally scrolled through birthdays, anniversaries, and holidays trying to make a connection. "No. What is it?"

"It will be 40 days. You will have been on the road 40 days— like Moses's 40 years in the wilderness in search of the Promised Land."

"Oh, my," I said in a whisper. "I never made the connection."

"We've really missed you, honey. I didn't want to make too big a point of it before now because I knew it would influence your decision to come home. I wanted you to take as much time as you needed. But I can't wait to see you."

*　*　*

I wanted to make one quick last side trip to Put-in-Bay, Ohio. Its name intrigued me. It was a nearby cluster of out-islands in Lake Erie. But heavy rains and fog reduced marine visibility to zero and the ferry was closed for the season. After mindlessly watching a few die-hard fishermen clean their catch at an outdoor fish-cleaning station, I headed for Michigan.

*　*　*

The crackling fire in the inn's fireplace was a welcome sight, given the weather outside. The Great Room was filled with antiques, overstuffed chairs, magazines, and board games. I couldn't wait to curl up in front of the fire after dinner with my journal and summarize a few final thoughts about life on the road. It never happened.

After a lovely dinner, I paced the living room unable to concentrate. The exhausting travel day and my racing thoughts about the return home sabotaged any serious pondering. I went to bed. I would have the rest of my life to sort out the trip.

The next morning a loud uneasy roar jolted me awake. Over breakfast, our cheery host explained it was the waves pounding the high sand dunes nearby, along the eastern shores of Lake Michigan.

On the Chicago side of Lake Michigan, the waters are typically tranquil. But this time of year on the eastern shore, she said, the lake's temperament borders on manic. I wolfed down breakfast and bundled up to go take a closer look.

Wild, undulating waves thundered toward land with frightening intensity. I watched their raw display of power in silence, wondering what they might say to me on this 40th day if they had a voice.

They'd probably say, "Stop waiting for the planets to align into some grand life plan. You know enough. You know more about who you are than you did when you started. You've clarified what's important. Start moving toward something that will pull you into the future with joy and hope, even if you don't know how it will all turn out. Just do it. And live like you mean it!

Sometimes the quest to understand leaves us stuck, looking at our shoes. It doesn't move us forward, dissolve our fears, or remove the obstacles in our path. It's life on a trickle charge. I was done watching life and ready to live again.

I didn't notice the icy waters lapping over my shoes until my feet went numb.

* * *

The drive around the southern tip of Lake Michigan took only a couple of hours. I flew north off I-80 toward the Chicago Skyway without noticing a big drop in the posted speed limit. Revolving mars lights appeared in my rearview mirror.

A Chicago cop approached my car with a bored, lumbering gait. He was right out of Central Casting, complete with scowl and beer belly.

"May I see your driver's license, ma'am."

I handed over my license, unaware I was stupidly grinning like a hippie on a different kind of trip.

"What so funny?"

"Nothing, officer. Not a thing." Then, involuntarily, I burst out laughing.

"Hey, lady, have you been drinking? Do you think this is funny?"

"I'm sorry," I said. "I've been away from my family for six weeks and I'm almost home!" I did a raucous stadium stomp on the floor of my car. "Whoo, hoo!"

He looked at my license and then at me, trying to decide if I was drunk or crazy or both. No matter how hard I tried to look less idiotic, I couldn't stop the goofy grinning. Then the laughter started again and this time I couldn't stop.

After what seemed like an eternity, he handed back my license as the tiniest of grins began to cross his face.

"Well, anybody that happy better get home and get off the street before the rest of us catch what you've got. Get out of here! But tell your foot not to be so happy on the accelerator the rest of the way home, okay?"

He shook his head in disbelief that he was letting me off the hook, then walked back to his car and pulled away.

As I crossed the Skyway, the skyline came into view. Chicago never looked so beautiful. I turned on the radio and, remarkably, the same country song by Alabama that I heard the day I left Chicago came on the air again:

> "I'm always in a hurry to get things done.
> I rush and I rush until life's no fun.
> All I really gotta do is live and die,
> But I'm always in a hurry and I don't know why."

Not anymore, baby! Not anymore!

Chapter 17

"I have learned the hard way that some
poems don't rhyme and some stories don't
have a clear beginning, middle, and end.
I have learned that life is about not
knowing and having to change. I have
discovered that life is filled with ambiguity.
Delicious ambiguity."

Gilda Radner
It's Always Something

THE FAT LADY SINGS

Once home, I quickly settled back into a comfortable routine, easing out of consulting into what I hoped would be a kinder, gentler life as a freelance writer, with a few consulting projects on the side to help pay the bills. George read my trip journal over the next couple weeks and we talked for hours about what the trip meant for our future.

"You have to write about this, you know," he said. " It would be criminal not to do so."

"I didn't take the trip in order to write a book, remember? We agreed there would be no pressure to 'make something' out of the trip."

"I know. But what you learned could help other people. This is stuff everyone struggles with. You can't keep it to yourself."

"I don't know. It feels disingenuous to turn it into a book."

"But that's what writers do. They write about what they know. Besides, it's *your* story. No one else can tell it."

"I know, but I'm not sure I want to be that self-revelatory. I like my privacy."

"Think about the books you've read that spoke deeply to you. They weren't dry academic discussions about life. They were personal stories where the author 'put himself out there,' warts and all."

"I'll think about it. But no promises! First, I want to see if what I learned on the road takes root in my heart and holds up in real life."

*   *   *

Eighteen months later the bottom fell out of my world. I never saw it coming. My husband George, the man who championed my dreams, decided he couldn't do marriage anymore. I knew he was going through a tough season. We talked about it all the time. But one day something in him snapped.

My trip had nothing to do with it. There was no "other woman." Rather, his chronic health issues worsened dramatically. His struggling business—a success for 25 years—was on life support and headed for its demise. And his beloved mentally challenged brother, for whom he was guardian, died. It was a trifecta of grief.

He became reclusive and paranoid and began making poor decisions. We separated, he moved in with his daughter, and promised to get help. I hoped the separation would be temporary. Then one day he showed up unannounced with movers to take all his belongings, saying, "...until we get things sorted out."

Intuitively, I knew he had given up.

A few days later I called him to see how he was doing. His daughter said he was gone...as in *really gone*, off the grid. All she knew was that he was holed up somewhere in a remote location in the San Bernardino Mountains in California, address unknown. I had no idea why he picked that location. To my knowledge, he had never been anywhere near there. He had set up a post office box in a nearby town to receive any urgent mail, but only one person had the address and it wasn't me. He didn't want me to know where he was or how to find him.

About five months later he returned to his daughter's home and called to say he wanted a divorce.

"We had something wonderful—a smiling-all-night-long insane kind of love that some people never experience," he said. "But love isn't enough to guarantee a good marriage. Marriage is made of different stuff and I don't have it. I'm glad we had what we had, but I can't do it anymore."

He said he was thinking of moving to someplace remote and warmer, where he could live frugally and paint. "It's what I was born to do."

*   *   *

As word spread to our circle of friends, the questions piled up: "What happened? What *really* happened? Was it a nervous breakdown? What did he say? What did *you* say? How do you feel? What are you going to do?"

Beyond the bare-bones facts, I said little. What little I knew made no sense and sounded like a tall tale that strained credulity. So what good would more information have been? In the end, I was left to speculate about a lot of it, along with everyone else. It was not a scenario I could have imagined in my wildest dreams. The man with a genius IQ and a photographic memory, who had tried cases before the Illinois Supreme Court, had lost his way and closed the path behind him.

Those who mattered most to me pulled me into their protective circle. Weeks passed. I would stare out the living room window for hours, revisiting every event since we had met, searching for clues to what might have produced a different outcome. Counseling and the support of family and friends kept me putting one foot in front of the other.

I didn't think I could support myself with just my freelance writing, so I continued my business consulting, too. Angels must have been deployed on my behalf, because it was the most productive consulting season of my life, despite a crippling depression and a shattered self-confidence. Fear of failure is also a great motivator.

One day I adopted a dog, a beautiful Greater Swiss Mountain Dog whose owner had recently died from cancer. The woman's family said the dog was grieving and, therefore, might not be herself at first. That made two of us. I knew we'd get along just fine.

I took up tennis, sorted through old files, planted flowers, and wallpapered the kitchen—anything to feel alive until I found a pulse.

It wasn't until I caught myself going through closets, frantically turning all the hangers in the same direction that I realized what the manic activity was about. I thought I could outrun the pain. Filling every inch of life with activity only delayed the healing. I needed to face the pain and deal with it.

I began to cry and didn't stop crying for a week. I cried in counseling. I cried with friends, at church, and around family. I cried walking down the produce aisle at the supermarket and sitting in the photography class I was taking to get my mind onto something more positive. Mostly I wept alone in my living room, face down in the carpet with my precious dog hunkered down beside me, as if to keep me warm until help arrived.

Deep into the grief, I realized I was crying for more than the loss of George. It was about my life and the years spent trying to make sure everything was perfect and under control. Being perfect is a terrible burden. It drove me to try every formula and strategy and mantra under the sun to get life right. But, in the end, it was a fool's errand.

The life I wanted wasn't "out there" waiting for me to find it's exact location—that magic spot that represented my place in the world, the place where everything would suddenly make sense.

And it definitely didn't require the perfect job or looks or marital status.

The clues had been right under my nose all along—inextricably linked to my personality, the things I feel passionate about, the things I love to do and do well because they reflected my natural gifts, and my yearning to fully become the woman God intended me to be before I decided he needed some help.

God harnesses all those clues to a vision. Then he protects the vision with spiritual values that he created expressly for the journey. He plants them in our hearts, waiting for us to access them.

It sounded too easy. It felt like a trick. Shouldn't it be harder? I thought I had to fight for it and that only a chosen few were ever destined to find it.

I was wrong.

God has a million ways to use us to make a difference in the world. He has a universe to run and needs our help. The problem is that we aren't paying attention. And we can't imagine He means *us*.

That's probably why a true understanding of meaning and purpose doesn't come to us in a flash of blinding light in some mountaintop experience. Rather, it trickles down to us in inklings—a word spoken by a friend, an anecdote in a book, an awakening about who we are and what might be possible if we dare to place our lives in the hands of a creative God—the One who does not jump to our tune but who has a finer song in mind for us.

When we finally see God and our lives through a lens cleansed of the cultural "gunk" that clouds our sight, we can see that he knows what he's doing and…somehow…will get us across the finish line. We can finally believe that life is safer with him than any of the alternatives.

Giving up control and trusting someone else—even God—is hard for people like me to whom life has not always been kind.

Trusting God is more like an uneasy truce. I suspect He's okay with that. He wants me to make it and He knows I'm doing the best I can.

* * *

The divorce was final two weeks before Christmas. I sold the house, bought a townhouse 35 miles away, found a new church, and signed up for a divorce recovery workshop. In counseling, I worked to change self-defeating behaviors that attracted people into my life that weren't good for me. Inch by inch, life trickled back into my bones.

To my surprise, the following spring George called out of the blue.

"I've realized some things I thought you deserved to know," he said. "When I married you I never meant to harm you. I thought I had something to offer—something that would be good for you. But I began to feel I was a millstone around your neck with my chronic illness, modest income, and all the rage that started to seep out from old emotional baggage. I couldn't stand the pain of knowing what I was doing to you and I didn't know how to stop it. An 'amputation' of sorts seemed like the only way to end the emotional pain. I'm sorry. I know I've wronged you. I just wanted you to know."

* * *

As I cast about for a new starting line for my life, I kept returning to the trip. It had been a liberating, defining season, exposing my weaknesses and reaffirming my gifts. The faces of those I met kept recycling through my mind—the people who had faced their pain and survived, as well as those who had given up. Duck Man reinvented his life after life-threatening brain surgery. The motel maid and gas station couple in Fall Creek Falls used their vision of the future to slog through a tedious "present."

On the other hand, the couple that ran the general store and the teacher in the Laundromat seemed shackled to their despair. So many stories to draw from, a library of wisdom to mull. I wondered what their stories might have to say about what I was now going through.

I picked up the manuscript about the trip that I had started when I first returned home and began to write again.

Then one day—a date I didn't note or memorialize—I knew I had turned a corner.

I was listening to a speaker talk about failure. To commit to a life of growth, he said, was to accept repeated experiences of fear and failure. The key is to look on them as events, not judgments about your life. The end of your story is still unwritten.

*   *   *

To be born with a question in both cheeks is both a blessing and a curse. It guarantees an interesting life, but you can never leave things alone. Everything must be held up to the light and *examined* and *scrutinized* and *explained* and *understood* before it can be released.

Well…usually.

Of all the wisdom I gained from the road, learning to live with unanswered questions may have been the most important lesson of all.

This messy, uneven, fractured thing we call life is a gift, a canvas to be explored. It cannot be tamed. Artists and writers and musicians know this. They never know how their paintings or stories or music will end when they begin, but they begin anyway—eager to participate in the unfolding miracle that is *their story*.

This is my story. Now go find yours. Your moment has not passed. If you're willing, God will find you and take you where you need to be.

Then one day—a day when you least expect it—a smile will break out and overwhelming gratitude will well up in you and you'll know. *This is it. This is the life with my name on it. Finally, I'm home.*

"So don't we all love a wild girl
keeping a hold on a dream she wants." [1]

From "Gone"
By Carl Sandburg

---

[1] Carl Sandburg, "Gone," *Selected Poems,* (New York, Gramercy Books, 1992), 160

Made in the USA
Columbia, SC
13 March 2019